INSIGHT COMPACT GUIDE

CW00385894

Compact Guide: Toronto is the ultimate quick-reference guide to Canada's megacity. It tells you everything you need to know about Toronto's attractions, from the heights of the CN Tower to the delights of Queen Street, from the elegance of Queens Park to the bustle of Chinatown.

This is one of more than 100 titles in Insight Guides' series of pocket-sized, easy-to-use guidebooks edited for the independent-minded traveller. Compact Guides are in essence travel encyclopedias in miniature, designed to be comprehensive yet portable, as well as up-to-date and authoritative.

Star Attractions

An instant reference
to some of
Toronto's top
attractions to help
you set your
priorities.

*St James' Cathedral
p18*

New City Hall p22

Sky Pod view p25

Elgin Theatre p21

Chinatown p27

*Art Gallery of
Ontario p30*

Queen Street West p32

*Royal Ontario
Museum p38*

Island cottages p49

The Beaches p50

Niagara Falls p58

TORONTO

Introduction

Places

Culture

Leisure

Practical Information

Toronto – The Place of Meeting

Described in *Fortune* magazine as 'the best international city for work and family' and as an 'urban miracle' by *Newsweek*, Toronto has come a long way from its humble Indian-village prehistoric origins. Although for the past few decades it has steadily earned monikers from the word go – 'Toronto the good', 'Hogtown', 'Muddy York', to name a few – the city today defies the glib generalisations that it once garnered.

Toronto's name stems from the Huron Indian word *turuntu*, meaning 'place of meeting'. So-called because this region was where, from around 1000BC, the trading routes between Lake Ontario, Lake Huron and Georgian Bay converged, the city has lived up to its name ever since. It has been a mecca for First Nations communities, French exploration, British colonisation, American occupation and waves of multi-ethnic immigration – all within a span of a couple of hundred years.

The CN Tower

5

Toronto has managed to shed its uptight Victorian past and emerge as a city of superlatives – superlatives that include the world's tallest building (the CN Tower) and the world's longest street (Yonge). Abuzz with culture, entertainment and big business, it has seen meteoric economic growth in the past 20 years. The city accommodates more internationally top-ranked companies than any other Canadian city, enjoys an accessibility to key markets and has forged solid links to the global economy.

Culturally, Toronto is headlined as the world's third most important theatre centre (after New York and London), with a smattering of historic theatres offering everything from blockbuster musicals to alternative, indigenous plays. Other performing arts are alive and well too: the Toronto Symphony Orchestra has the largest subscription audience in the continent, and the city is ranked third (in terms of output) in North America for film and video production, with up to 40 productions being shot here on any given day.

Music while you walk

But it is still a place where tiny Victorian buildings sit next to towering skyscrapers and grassy parks battle it out with ever-encroaching pavement. In short, it is a city of contradiction: a backwater that has been infused with urban glut; a muddy-streeted shadow of British intention that is now the glamorous independent, but of a very different ilk from an American city of the same size.

With over 4,000 restaurants, hundreds of theatres, galleries and museums, close to 400 parks and a calendar rife with festivals, the city provides untrammelled ground for those looking to explore its diverse offerings.

Toronto at night

The city and its islands

Summer on the boardwalk

Location and size

Hugging the northwest shore of Lake Ontario, Toronto lies further south than much of Michigan and all of Minnesota, and shares the same latitude as the California-Oregon border. Lake Ontario, the smallest of the Great Lakes, is 311km (259 miles) long and 244m (805ft) at its deepest point. A little over half of the lake's total area lies on the Ontario side of the border shared with New York State. In fact, on a clear day, from some of the city's skyscrapers and the CN Tower, it is possible to glance across the lake to Rochester, New York.

The map of Toronto has been described as a Christmas tree, with Yonge Street as its tall trunk. Yonge serves as the central, north-south thoroughfare supporting the main east-west streets, which include Queen Street, Dundas Street, Bloor Street and Eglington Avenue. Speckled throughout the city are neighbourhoods and ethnic enclaves, each with their own cultural distinction and hub of activity.

The city extends beyond the shore and incorporates the series of 18 islands known as the Toronto Islands. An eastern peninsula that was separated from the mainland by successive storms that swept through the area in the 1850s, the islands can be reached by a 10-minute ferry ride, and are home to one of the city's two major airports, the Toronto City Centre Airport.

Climate

Like most of Canada, Toronto undergoes a deep transformation from season to season. Although the weather is touted as being about the mildest in Canada, that is scant consolation for those who find themselves in the clutches of a fierce January snowstorm. Thankfully, the city is blessed with lots of sunshine during all seasons. Toronto's proximity to Lake Ontario is also a benefit; a welcome modifier, it keeps the city warmer during the winter months, while acting as a coolant during the summer.

Summers can get hot, but generally temperatures average around 23°C (73°F), making for pleasant sightseeing weather. Still, it is difficult to muster up enthusiasm for traipsing around the city in the thick of a summer heatwave, so when things hot up, many flock to the offshore breezes of the Beaches district and the Toronto Islands.

Conversely, winters are cool (with an average temperature of -6°C/21°F) and can get bitterly cold. Snow is usually minimal, but occasionally snowfalls can be so heavy that they disrupt traffic. When snow blankets the city, it dampens all noise, giving a strange tranquillity to a normally hectic urban landscape.

With everything abloom in May and the leaves ablaze by late October, fall and spring are the prettiest times of year. The sunny, warm days and crisp, cool nights of these seasons are also conducive to strolling around the city.

Population

At 4.6 million people, the population of Toronto has more than doubled since 1971. Roughly 14 percent of Canada's citizens live here, though the city occupies a mere 0.006 percent of its land.

A true polyglot, the population represents over 80 ethnic groups speaking over 100 languages. With the largest single group representing approximately one-fifth of the people and over a dozen cultural groups having more than 100,000 members, the days of a single majority culture are no longer. Instead, the city is a colourful weave of ethnic diversity which brings a vibrant mix of culture, resplendent in everything from food and fashion, to festivals and music. Here you will find the largest Portuguese community in North America, one of the largest Italian communities outside Italy, and a little India and Greektown teeming with food and wares from their respective homelands – not to mention several Chinatowns.

Italian vendors
Indian lady

From metro to megacity

The city of Toronto used to fall under the heading Metro Toronto, but in 1998 an act of the provincial parliament dissolved the boundaries of Toronto, Scarborough, North York, Etobicoke, York and East York, merging the city with its satellites. This was a cost-saving measure, replacing the local municipal and metropolitan governments with a new City of Toronto.

The amalgamation was opposed by the gamut of citizens, from the city's artists and literati, to media and economic pundits. World-renowned writer Michael Ondaatje pronounced it a 'case of democracy being eliminated by fiat', while the city's economists predicted a precipitous

The new megacity

raise in property taxes. The fight over the amalgamation of Toronto city, Canada's first metropolitan government, with its neighbours was seen as the fight against marginalization of the citizen's voice.

Economically, the proposition sparked opposing views. On the one hand, it was considered to be the downloading of responsibility for social welfare on to local property tax, while on the other, Ontario's Premier touted it as having the potential to forge a city with the most financial and political clout in the country. Regardless, the idea of the 'urban monolith' raised the question of the nature of community, as Toronto has been, in essence, a collection of villages and neighbourhoods of distinct and vibrant cultures – and continues to be so today.

Despite opposition, the amalgamation has gone ahead, earning Toronto the title of 'megacity' and transforming it into the fourth-largest city in North America.

Economy

Toronto is *the* monetary capital of Canada. With a strong financial services sector, a focus on high technology and the availability of a labour force with specialist skills, the city is a natural locus for financial activity. Toronto is also home to over 75,000 businesses and the country's highest count of internationally top-ranked companies. Canada's major banks, 90 percent of its foreign banks, upper-echelon investment dealers, and half of the country's largest insurance companies maintain their corporate headquarters here.

Looking up from Bay Street

Stock Market Place

The heart of the city's financial district is Bay Street, Canada's equivalent of New York's Wall Street. Here, the Toronto Stock Exchange (TSE) ranks as the third largest by value and the second by volume in North America. A whopping 75 percent of the money invested in Canadian stocks flows through the TSE.

In the manufacturing sector, Toronto's economy is intertwined with the automobile industry, along with heavy equipment, iron and steel, chemical products and electronics. The majority of the bigger factories sit outside the city in an area that has been given the sobriquet The Golden Horseshoe, due to its great earning power. Tourism, and the new industry of eco-tourism, also play a large part in enriching the local economy, having both mushroomed in the last decade.

Nature and environment

The city is generously flecked with green spaces, even within its downtown core. Early records of the area talk of stands of gigantic red and white pines growing on the hills engulfing the Don River, which itself was once laden with oversized pink salmon and surrounded by thick gooseberry bushes. As little as 150 years ago, wolves, deer, black bear, elk, wolverine, marten, bobcats, muskrats and waterfowl lived off the fertile riverbeds and forests that now comprise the city of Toronto.

Although a far cry from the dramatic ecological splendour from which it sprang, Toronto has managed to maintain a sizable number of public parks and small green areas (386 to be exact). The waterfront is skirted by a green band that runs from beyond the Toronto Islands to the 100m (300ft)-high Scarborough Bluffs at the east end of the waterfront. Further west is the Beaches district, with its lakeside boardwalk that snakes through a string of waterside parks. At the foot of Leslie Street, the Leslie Street Spit, formerly known as Tommy Thompson Park, is a great place to watch birds: over 185 species, mainly water birds, make this area home.

Cows in the city: sculptures at the Dominion Centre

Abundant parks, ponds and beaches can be found on the Toronto Islands, where a school of natural science also resides. The islands are operated by the Toronto Parks and Culture Department which has ensured that no cars are allowed in this ecologically sensitive area. Instead, bikes, roller blades, canoes and sailboats are the modes of transport here.

9

Within the city there are any number of grassy nooks in which to take a moment to grab a quiet respite, including the ever-exotic Allan Gardens on the edge of the Cabbagetown district. This 5.2-hectare (13-acre) park is a botanical delight, with lush greenery and extensive greenhouses open to the public year round. On the other side of the city, High Park (which starts at the corner of Bloor Street West and Parkside Drive and extends all the way south to The Queensway) is one of Toronto's biggest parks, replete with lush gardens, Grenadier Pond, bike paths and a small zoo.

Recreation on Centre Island

Historical Highlights

pre 1600s Archaeologists have uncovered evidence revealing at least 6,000 years of human activity in the region. For these thousands of years, the routes between Lake Ontario, Lake Huron and Georgian Bay converge at Toronto, stemming from the native Huron word *turuntu*, meaning 'place of meeting'.

1615 Etienne Brûlé, a French explorer, is the first white man to see all the Great Lakes and discovers the native village of Teiaiagon, on the site of what is now Toronto.

1640–90 The 'Carrying-Place' (Toronto's location posited it as the portage link between Lake Ontario and the Upper Lakes) is visited by Dutch and British traders from New York, along with French explorers and priests.

1720 The French establish the first trading post, trading fur with the Mississauga Indians.

1750 Fort Toronto (also called Rouillé) is built by the French.

1759 The French defeat at the Quebec City Battle of the Plains of Abraham eventually leads to the British winning control of the whole Great Lakes region.

1787 Known as the 'Toronto Purchase', the British buy approximately 480 sq km (400 sq miles) from the Mississauga First Nations for the sum of £1,700, 149 barrels of flour and other goods such as blankets and axes.

1793 Colonel John Graves Simcoe, the first lieutenant-governor of Upper Canada, chooses Toronto as the place of operations for naval defence against the Americans, due to the vantage point it offers. Along with building a garrison, Fort York, he also sets out a 10-block plan for the town, thus establishing the north-south, east-west road grid the city retains to this day. In addition, Simcoe sheds the city's age-old aboriginal association by changing Toronto's name to York – in honour of the Duke of York's victory over the French revolutionary armies.

1812 The War of 1812. Naval skirmishes are fought for control of Lakes Erie and Ontario.

1813 York's military strength is tested when, during the spring, 1,700 Americans take the fort in a matter of hours. They subsequently loot and burn much of the little town, including the parliament buildings. York is retaken by the British 11 days later.

1824 William Lyon Mackenzie's *Colonial Advocate* begins publication and soon becomes Upper Canada's most popular newspaper. The same year marks the opening of the Welland Canal, which links Lake Erie and Lake Ontario, making the town an important trade centre along the Montreal-Chicago shipping axis.

1829–34 In just five years, the influx of British and Irish immigrants causes York's population to quadruple to almost 10,000.

1834 The town of York is renamed the city of Toronto. In March, William Lyon Mackenzie is chosen as the first mayor.

1837 Ironically, Toronto's first mayor goes on to lead an unsuccessful rebellion against the predominantly Tory rule only three years after being elected into office. Campaigning for municipal service and reform, the Mackenzie Rebellion lasts two days, with two of the leaders ending up hanged.

1841 Upper and Lower Canada are reorganised as the United Province of the Canadas, and the capital is moved from Toronto to Kingston.

1843 King's College, later to be the University of Toronto, opens its doors.

1844 Editor-politician George Brown, a future premier and Toronto's own father of Confederation, founds the *Globe*, which starts as a radical journal but later becomes the voice of Toronto Liberal businessmen.

1847 Around 40,000 Irish refugees fleeing the potato famine in their homeland arrive, boosting the already burgeoning Irish communities.

1850 The construction of the Gothic St James Cathedral begins. At one point, it enjoys the distinction of being North America's tallest spire.

1853 The arrival of the railway brings an end to Toronto's reliance on ships and wagons – both limited by winter weather – for transporting goods and resources over long distances. The first influx of Asian immigrants come with the building of these railroads.

1857 The sand bar connecting the mainland to the peninsula is opened up in a storm, forming a new entrance to the harbour and creating Toronto Island (later renamed Centre Island).

1867 Under The Confederation of Canada, Toronto becomes the new capital of the recently created province of Ontario.

1878 The Canadian National Exhibition, the world's largest annual fair, is opened.

1879 University of Toronto's Sir Stanford Flemming is credited as inventing Standard Time.

1884 North America's first electric streetcar makes its debut in the Canadian National Exhibition (CNE) grounds.

1901 Toronto's population exceeds 300,000.

1904 More than 100 buildings are demolished in a fire that sweeps through the downtown core, changing the look of these historic neighbourhoods for ever.

1906 The name 'Toronto the Good' is coined after the Lord's Day legislation, which prohibits various types of entertainment.

1911 Sir Henry Pellatt begins work on his fated home, later to be named Casa Loma, complete with turrets and secret passageways – ostensibly Toronto's only castle. With the price tag for its construction a whopping $3.5 million, and increasing financial troubles, Pellatt is forced to abandon his castle. Opened briefly as a hotel, the building is seized in 1937 as a tourist attraction and has been open to the public ever since.

1921 While working at the University of Toronto, Dr Frederick Banting discovers insulin, the hormone responsible for diabetes.

1929 This year of extremes sees both the decadence of the opening of the Royal York Hotel (at the time the largest hotel in the British Empire), then the rock-bottom poverty created by the stock market's Great Crash on Black Thursday (24 October). As almost a third of the city's residents are rendered unemployed, the Great Depression takes hold.

1931 Maple Leaf Gardens is constructed. Home to the Toronto Maple Leafs hockey team and a notable gathering place, this arena currently faces permanent closure.

1934 The Toronto Stock Exchange moves into what is Canada's first air-conditioned building, at 234 Bay Street.

1938 Malton Airport (later to be named Pearson International Airport) is opened. It is now the busiest airport in the country.

1939 War is brought close to home after 200 Toronto citizens are killed when the ocean liner *Athenia* is destroyed by a German torpedo.

1947 First cocktail bars are allowed in Toronto.

1954 Canada's first subway line opens in Toronto. Hurricane Hazel wreaks havoc on the city, with damages estimated at $25 million and over 80 people killed.

1959 The multimillion-dollar St Lawrence Seaway, connecting Lake Ontario with the Atlantic ocean, is opened.

1970s Faced with cultural and economic uncertainty, Anglo-Quebeckers from Montreal begin to relocate to Toronto in droves.

1976 The much-anticipated CN Tower opens, enjoying the title of the world's tallest free-standing structure.

1989 The SkyDome, the first stadium in the world with a retractable roof, is opened.

1993 The Toronto Blue Jays baseball team clinches its second World Series title.

1998 Metro Toronto is abolished, and the previous annexed areas are amalgamated into one 'megacity'. Former North York mayor Mel Lastman is elected mayor of the new city, which now ranks as the fourth-largest city in the whole of North America.

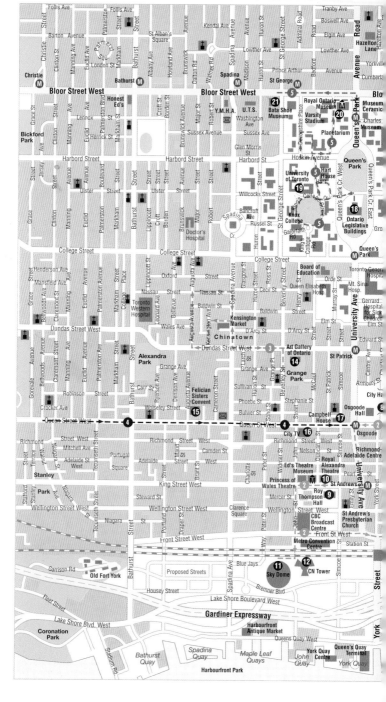

ROUTES 1–6

| 0 | 600 m |
| 0 | 600 yards |

St Lawrence Market

Tour 1

St Lawrence Neighbourhood

St Lawrence Market – Front Street Shops and Buildings – St James Cathedral – St Lawrence Hall *See map on pages 14–15*

Once the heart of Toronto's commercial district, this historic neighbourhood has a lot to offer. From soaking up the eclectic architecture, to drinking in the atmosphere of a bustling market, to simply walking along exploring the many shops that dot Front and King Streets, the St Lawrence area evokes Toronto's history as well as providing a snapshot of this vibrant modern city.

Butchers at the market

A good starting point is the historic ★★ **St Lawrence Market ❶**, a cornucopia of sights, smells and sounds (at the intersection of Front Street East and Lower Jarvis Street, Tuesday to Thursday, 8am–6pm, Friday 8am–5pm, Saturday 5am–5pm). The building itself is a giant yet tidy structure that was the City Hall from 1845 to 1899. Its rear facade was uncovered to create the historical set for the modern-day market. Filling the two-storey building are endless stalls occupied by butchers, bakers and fishmongers. A smattering of ethnic foods adds to the culinary diversity, but basic foodstuffs are also plentiful. Stalls specialising in everything from Greek olives to Jarlsberg and Gouda cheeses, as well as fresh seafood, homemade pasta, spices and coffees, abound. Prepared food is available to eat on the spot or take on a picnic, making lunchtime and Saturday an extremely busy time.

For a sense of the history of the market and the surrounding area, visit the **Market Gallery** (95 Front Street

East, tel: 416-392-7604, Wednesday to Friday 10am–4pm, Saturday 9am–4pm, Sunday noon–4pm). The gallery is on the second floor (accessible via the elevator by the Front Street entrance), which during its City Hall days was a council chamber. Run by the City of Toronto Archives, it features photographs, maps, writings and artefacts from Toronto's past, and is free of charge.

Directly across the street is the **Farmers' Market**, difficult to miss with its colourful mural emblazoned on to the building's outer bricks. In 1803, Lieutenant-Governor Peter Hunter declared this area the marketplace, and Saturday market day. Ever since, farmers of southern Ontario have flocked to this long-established oxymoron – a rural marketplace functioning in an urban locale.

Farmers' produce and mural

Right next door to the Farmers' Market, and along the same vein, is the bright-blue painted brick of one of Toronto's longest-standing fish eateries, the Old Fish Market – providing yet another lunch option in an area chock-a-block with good places to eat (*see below*).

A left turn leads to **The Esplanade**, which was a misnomer until the street metamorphosed from railway-obstructed waterfront road to the adjunct of a more upscale, lakeside neighbourhood. The run-down warehouses have been restored and the upper floors are now home to a variety of architecture and design firms, publishing houses and other style-conscious offices, with oversized pubs, restaurants and cafés taking over street level. Some of the city's stock eating establishments can be found here, among them the ever-popular Organ Grinder, the Old Spaghetti Factory; or the Muddy York and Scotland Yard if watering holes are more your *modus operandi*. Although gourmet cuisine is scarce, many of these establishments spill outside on to patios in the summer months, creating a lively atmosphere for a drink or a quick bite.

Return towards Front Street East along Church Street to explore a string of outdoor outfitting shops in the section of Front Street East between the St Lawrence Market and Scott Street. Other shops housed in roomy restored buildings along this strip include Freida, with its mélange of Asian and South American houseware, clothing and jewellery, and the well-established Nicholas Hoare bookstore whose hardwood floors, high ceilings and tall wooden bookshelf-reaching ladders conjure up dusty literary charm. Also here is the trendy **Toronto Life Café**, affiliate of the city's official lifestyle magazine of the same name, and a place to have a latté and read back issues.

Toronto Life Café

When you cross the road to **Berczy Park**, you get a beautiful view of the aforementioned shops, which are all housed in statuesque 19th-century buildings whose fanciful facades echo the bustling commercial street that was

Derek Besant's Flat Iron Mural

St James' spire and organ detail

once the city's economic hub. The park itself occupies the lower half of the triangular block created by the intersection of Front Street East and takes its name from one of Canada's finest early portrait painters, William Berczy.

Adjacent stands the **Gooderham Building** of the distillery-owning Gooderhams. It began as a flour mill but had so many payments made in grain by struggling farmers that the company decided to convert them into alcohol, which it sold. By 1877, the Gooderham and Worts Distillery became the largest in the world. Today the building flaunts the playful **Flat Iron Mural**, of a windowed building rendered to look like a painting with curling edges nailed into the brick, by contemporary artist Derek Besant.

From Berczy Park, head north on the aptly named Church Street. This little stretch on Church and neighbouring Bond Streets contains St Michael's Catholic Cathedral, the 'Cathedral of Methodism', the first Lutheran Church and St George's Greek Orthodox Church.

Across King Street towers the spire of ★★★ **St James' Cathedral ❷** (106 King Street East). Built between 1849 and 1853, this sober cathedral proclaimed its ties to the British homeland with English Gothic architecture that was, and still is, utterly dignified. The building that stands today is the fourth St James' Cathedral on the site, which was started after the Great Fire of 1849 had destroyed its predecessor. The cathedral's 100-m (306-ft) spire, the tallest in Canada, was once the tallest in North America. The interior evokes equal drama, with its elaborate hammerbeam ceiling, Queen Anne organ cases and a stained-glass window by Tiffany & Co of New York (*circa* 1900). Cushioning the cathedral from urban encroachment is the surrounding St James' Park, a delightful, recreated, 19th-century garden.

The **King Edward Hotel** (37 King Street East) was built in 1901 and even then held an air of dignity amid the crowded streetscape. The hotel was largely responsible for bucking an anti-social trend on the part of the upper-middle classes of Toronto to shun dining out or entertaining away from home. The King Edward's regal design gave it a social cachet that society's élite were looking for. Although since modified, the expensive European restaurant, now known as the Victoria Café, is still replete with a decadently lavish interior: an extravagant Edwardian version of Louis XV style with lace curtains, velvet draperies, panels hung with brocade silk framed in rococo mouldings, with a ceiling dripping with crystal chandeliers. It has been said that this hotel most symbolises the lifestyle and standards of a period that has all but vanished.

Situated at the intersection of Jarvis Street and King Street East is the opulent ★ **St Lawrence Hall ❸**. The

Victorian classicism, exemplified by the majestic Corinthian-columned front, prompts the building to stand out from its neighbours, yet its sheer functionality makes it blend in with the streetscape. Municipal offices, shops, a public market, an upscale Italian restaurant with a breezy patio, and a sumptuous 30m (100ft) banquet hall are all housed within. Punctuated by an elaborate plaster ceiling, gleaming crystal chandelier and gilt decoration, the Grand Hall has a long history of hosting gallant affairs. Now a popular locale for wedding receptions, it was here that Canada's first Prime Minister campaigned, and showman P.T. Barnum presented the famous dwarf Tom Thumb in his freak shows.

Drifting east from St Lawrence Hall along King Street, there is a variety of shops that specialise predominantly in architecture, interior design and visual arts. This is not surprising considering the area is imbued with older buildings that have been restored to house spacious offices for design-oriented professionals.

St Lawrence Hall

A stroll down the street reveals interior furnishing, lighting, framing, arts, crafts and antiques. Among these is **Arts on King** (169 King Street East), an emporium stocked with a large collection of art and crafts, jewellery, candle holders, unusual mirrors and other decorative items made by local artists.

Upstairs, the spacious **Wagner Rosenbaum Gallery** showcases an eclectic variety of paintings, sculpture and works in other media by emerging Canadian artists (listings for which can be found in city newspapers).

Continuing along this stretch makes for good design-oriented window shopping, with stores beginning to thin around Parliament Street. Catching a King Streetcar westbound returns you to the heart of the St Lawrence area.

Wagner Rosenbaum Gallery

Towers of metal and glass

Tour 2

Theatre and Financial District

Massey Hall – Elgin and the Winter Garden Theatres – Old City Hall – New City Hall & Nathan Phillips Square – Osgoode Hall – Roy Thompson Hall – Royal Alexandra Theatre – Princess of Wales Theatre – CBC Broadcast Centre – SkyDome – CN Tower – Union Station – Royal York – Hummingbird Centre – Hockey Hall of Fame *See map on pages 14–15*

The financial district from above...

...and below

Perhaps no other part of the city offers such a dramatic contrast of aesthetic and commercial sensibilities as Toronto's theatre and financial district. The title itself points out the oxymoron – a place where drama battles it out with the stock market and where skyscrapers dwarf the grandiose theatres of old. A glimpse down any of the streets demonstrates the benefits of architectural restoration: a mélange of 19th-century buildings adds dignity, beauty and a sense of past to the 20th-century glass and metal. The original metropolitan vision of Toronto was very European, with no skyscrapers (the first appeared in 1906). Church spires and elegant buildings have given way to mammoth modern structures, however, and the two now enjoy a precarious co-existence. In fact, today these are the structures that define the financial, business and civic core. But don't be deceived. This 'heart of Toronto' is far more than a financial outpost. It offers a wide variety of entertainment: blockbuster plays, a skate in Nathan Phillips Square or a trip up the world's tallest tower.

Starting out between Dundas and Queen on Yonge Street, your first encounter is a small pocket of some of Toronto's best-known performance venues. The **Pantages** (263 Yonge Street, tel: 416-872-2222), across from the Eaton Centre, has a checkered past. Originally built as a vaudeville house in 1920, it was later converted into a movie house when talking pictures began to elbow out live entertainment. After a number of attempted changes, it reopened in 1988, operating as a fully fledged theatre.

Walking south on to Shuter Street, just off Yonge sits **Massey Hall ❹** (15 Shuter Street, tel: 416-872-4255), Toronto's first permanent concert hall. Massey Music Hall as it was formerly called, was built between 1889 and 1894 as a gift to the city by farm-machinery magnate Hart Massey. Its rather sombre architecture was not helped by the addition of iron fire escapes in the 1930s, which conceal much of the building's original detail. Opened with an elaborate performance of Handel's *Messiah*, this Carnegie Hall-era venue is still renowned for its impeccable acoustics, and many world-famous musicians have, and still do, pass through its doors.

Massey Hall

Just south is the ★★ **Elgin and the Winter Garden Theatres ❺** (189 Yonge Street, tel: 416-314-2871), the only double-decker theatres still operating in the world. The Elgin (built in 1913) features Italian Renaissance-style plasterwork, gold leaf and red plush, echoing its days as a former vaudeville house of lavish opulence. Upstairs, the Winter Garden (1914) is the smaller but more exotic of the two, with a ceiling of real leaves, supporting columns in the form of tree trunks, and trellised walls. Converted to movie theatres and then closed, they were restored in 1989 by the Ontario Heritage Foundation. The theatres have been staging popular productions, including *Cats* and performance troupes such as *Stomp*, to full houses ever since and can also be seen on a guided tour.

Elgin Theatre detail

The Bay, at the corner of Yonge and Queen Street West, is the descendant of the Hudson's Bay Company, Canada's oldest trading firm. From this building, a westward walk along Queen leads to the ★★ **Old City Hall ❻** (60 Queen Street West). Like most of Toronto's 19th-century buildings, this was the result of an international competition won by native Torontonian E.J. Lennox in 1885. The building is no stranger to controversy: lawsuits were slapped on the architect for everything from going over budget to having the letters of his name etched into the stone below the eaves; and on the opening day, in September 1899, Mayor Johan Shaw had to defend the extravagant price-tag by pleading 'where no such monuments are found, the mental and moral natures of the people have not been above the faculties of the beasts'.

The Old City Hall

Once one of the most visible landmarks of downtown Toronto, the 86-m (285-ft) off-centre **clock tower** is still an ethereal sight at the end of Bay Street. It commands the attention of passers-by just as the building itself remains one of the city's most compelling testaments to late-Victorian architecture. Thanks to the charitable aid of the Friends of Old City Hall, the demolition that once seemed imminent is now unlikely.

The New City Hall

Like its predecessor, the ★★★ **New City Hall** ❼ (100 Queen Street West) is the product of an international competition, this time with Finnish architect Viljo Revell's daring neo-expressionist design winning out. It has been said that the most important project a city undertakes is the building of its city hall, and the New City Hall proves to be a strong civic symbol. In fact, a bird's-eye view of the structure – the domed council chamber and two curved towers of unequal height, all set upon a two-storey platform – reveal that it is shaped much like an eye, a symbol in Finland for the tradition of democracy.

Although it has always provoked civic pride, the building has also had its share of nay-sayers. Architectural icon Frank Lloyd Wright warned Toronto that it had a headstone for a grave that 'future generations will look at and say: "This marks the spot where Toronto fell".' Derogatory quips aside, the structure's sculptural quality allows it to be seen and understood as a symbol that will never be overpowered by the ever upward-creeping skyline.

Judging by the steady trickle of visitors through the doors, modernists have done something right, however, as function and form seem to be co-existing effortlessly. The lobby houses a large, detailed model of Toronto's downtown which serves as a useful orientation tool. Pamphlets detailing the city's sights and other points of interest are helpful, as is the City Hall bookstore, selling various guides, maps and souvenirs.

City Hall overlooks the whole of the east side of ★ **Nathan Phillips Square** ❽, a vast plaza conceived and designed on a grand scale by Viljo Revell, and named after the first Jewish major of Toronto, who was its sponsor. The large pool at its south end offers cooling fountains in the heat of the summer, then becomes a busy ice-skating rink in winter; and with benches, sculpture and a Peace Garden, the square offers a pleasant place to sit back and watch the world go by.

Nathan Phillips Square: the Peace Garden

The **Peace Garden** is centred around a small stone slab, which was constructed for Toronto's 150th anniversary in 1984. With one broken corner, it evokes remembrance of the destruction of war and voices the wish for world peace. Henry Moore's sculpture, *Three-Way Piece No. 2* (commonly known as *The Archer*), was a controversial addition in 1965. Eventually funded privately due to concerns that there would be an outcry if taxpayers' money was spent on the hefty price tag of an abstract sculpture,

Osgoode Hall library

the piece ironically seems almost inconsequential in modern-day Toronto.

A walk westwards on Queen Street leads to the classical old-world charm of **Osgoode Hall** (116-138 Queen Street West), the city's mainstay of the legal world. The hall was originally built (starting in 1829 and continuing sporadically until 1844) as headquarters of the Law Society of Upper Canada and named after the first chief justice of the province, William Osgoode. It still serves the society and the long-established Osgoode Hall Law School, but now houses the Supreme Court of Ontario as well. Three architectural firms had their hand in the design which blended surprisingly well: the building has been revered as a successful architectural hybrid. The central facade, ornamented with rooftop urns, has a Versailles-like garden front, while the glass-roofed court and pillared stairway resemble an Italian palazzo. The impressive iron fence, which gives the building a distinguished air compared to its neighbours, was actually used to keep out wandering cows, once a serious problem. Despite being the official home to the provincial courts since 1846, the building has been said to have the feel of a private club. Worth a visit and open to the public is the elegant library, with its 12-m (40-ft) vaulted ceilings and elaborate plasterwork, often touted as one of the most dignified rooms in Canada.

Turning left into University Avenue and continuing south until King Street West, you enter another segment of thriving theatre district. A lively cultural scene usually means good eateries, and this area is no exception. Stylish restaurants along King, Peter and John Streets caters for the hungry lunch and theatre-going crowds and enlivens what could be a backdrop of corporate formality.

★★ **Roy Thompson Hall** ❾ (60 Simcoe Street at the intersection with King Street West, tel: 416-872-4255),

The Hey Lucy Café on King Street West

Royal Alexandra Theatre

CBC Broadcast Centre

named after the newspaper magnate Baron Thompson Fleet, who was also the main financial backer, has evoked mixed feelings. A 12,121sq m (40,000sq ft) circle of mirror glass that sits right on top of the sidewalk, the building has been called 'arrogant' and a 'neo-expressionist extravaganza', among other things. The Toronto Symphony Orchestra and Mendelssohn Choir both call Roy Thompson Hall their home, yet despite the dramatic web-of-glass update, the acoustic excellence of Massey Hall (*see page 21*) has not been rivalled. Instead, by moving plastic discs in the ceiling, the new venue was designed to tailor acoustics to the type of music and instrumentation. The building's architect, Arthur Erickson, has also been credited with creating an optical illusion on a grand scale (the building is actually much larger than it appears from the outside).

Almost directly across the street from Roy Thompson Hall, is a Beaux-Arts legacy, the ★ **Royal Alexandra Theatre ❿** (260 King Street West). Built in 1889 as a music hall and then converted into a theatre in 1895, Royal Alexandra was rejuvenated in 1963 when larger-than-life Toronto entrepreneur Ed Mirvish purchased it and saved it from demolition. Today, it imports its shows, mainly from London and New York. Known as 'Honest Ed', Mirvish has been credited with single-handedly restoring theatre attendance in Toronto. With the theatre/restaurant strip's flashing lights and old-fashioned signs, the Mirvish legacy is destined to flash and flicker on, and keep reeling in the crowds.

The **Princess of Wales Theatre** (300 King Street West, tel: 416-872-1212) was built by his son, David Mirvish, and opened in 1993 with the bang of Broadway blockbuster *Miss Saigon*. The theatre's size actually owes itself to this production, as it was constructed to accommodate *Miss Saigon*'s famous helicopter. The building is spared the kitsch ornateness of Mirvish senior's other creations, however, with an elegant and refined interior.

Strolling south on John Street to Front Street West, you see the unmistakable shimmer of the ★ CBC **Broadcast Centre** (250 Front Street West, tel: 416-205-5574). This slick red and silver building has provoked controversy – as does the CBC television company itself among Canadians. To some, it is the thread that inextricably links the vast but sparsely populated country, giving Canada its cultural identity; to others, it is simply a financial drain. For a chance to catch the taping of a radio or television programme, go to the main lobby or the Glenn Gould studio, where a variety of musical shows are recorded.

At Front and John is the imposing duo of Toronto's most famous modern buildings: the ★★ **SkyDome ⓫** (1 Blue

Jays Way, tel: 416-341-2770) and the CN Tower. Taking ideas from the ancient Greeks and Romans and stepping them up to ultra-modern speed, the Sky Dome's sleek design includes the cachet of having the world's largest fully retractable roof. When in its closed position, a 30-storey building could fit under the roof, which consists of four panels that can open or close in just 20 minutes. Official home to the Toronto Blue Jays baseball team, the stadium is also open for one-hour tours seven days a week, for those who are curious about its design and building process.

Michael Snow's 'The Audience' at the Sky Dome

The ★★★ **CN Tower** ⓬ (301 Front Street West, tel: 416-360-8500, concourse daily 10am–10pm), is without doubt the city's most popular sight, attracting over two million visitors each year. To behold the view offered by the world's tallest building at just over 553m (1,815ft), head to the Sky Pod observation gallery (8am–11pm) two-thirds the way up, with its vertigo-inducing glass floor on the observation deck. The Sky Pod also houses the microwave broadcasting equipment that was the building's original *raison d'être*, but here you can also find the revolving restaurant, 360 (*see page 77*), and the Horizons Bar. Height junkies can ascend a further 33 storeys to the Space Deck for an additional fee. At the base of the tower there is a new complex of shops, a 300-seat restaurant, an IMAX theatre and a flight simulator.

The dizzy heights of the Sky Pod

Heading east along Front until York Street, you reach **Union Station** (65-75 Front Street West), an elegant structure that was completed in 1927 and saw Torontonians through the era of train travel. The classical-revival building is almost 257m (850ft) long with an extravagant vaulted ceiling and a floor of muted grey and pink Tennessee marble; and, with its opulent colonnade and great hall inside, it remains a majestic reminder of an era gone by. The station still figures very prominently as the terminal for the suburban commuter system, as well as being a stop on the subway system, actually making it busier today than when it was built.

Union Station

Across from Union Station on the north side of Front is the **Royal York Hotel** (100 Front Street, tel: 416-368-2511). This skyscraper-cum-chateau overlooking the railway has been called Canadian Pacific Railway's castle, an apt name considering that members of the Royal Family do often stay here. Also completed in 1927, the Royal York once enjoyed the distinction of being the largest hotel in the British Commonwealth.

The **Hummingbird Centre for the Performing Arts** ⓭ (1 Front Street East, tel: 416-393-7469 or 416-872-2262) is one block east of Union Station on the southeast corner of Front and Yonge. In 1960, then known as the O'Keefe, the theatre opened its doors for the first

The Hockey Hall of Fame

Oasis of green at the Dominion Centre

Design Exchange exhibit

time to a smash hit of *Camelot*, starring Julie Andrews, Richard Burton and Robert Goulet. The interior houses York Wilson's *Seven Lively Arts*, the largest mural in Canada at 30m by 4.5m (100ft by 15ft). The building's residents also include the National Ballet and the Canadian Opera Company, along with visiting performers from various arts. Unfortunately the sight lines and acoustics are mediocre, so to get the most from a performance the more expensive seats are recommended.

On the northwest corner of Yonge and Front, in the former Bank of Montreal building, is the **Hockey Hall of Fame** (30 Yonge Street, tel: 416-360-7765, Monday to Friday 10am–5pm; Saturday 9.30am–6pm, Sunday 10.30am–5pm). Although suffering from a serious case of commercialism, this is essential viewing for die-hard hockey fans, replete with all things hockey: memorabilia, artefacts, interactive games and yes, the Stanley Cup.

Back to the throes of the business district, BCE **Place**, a little north of the Hockey Hall of Fame, is home to countless corporations and law offices and has also attracted several good restaurants.

Exiting BCE Place at Bay and Front, you come to the **Royal Bank Plaza** (200 Bay Street at Front Street), whose two glittery triangular towers stand out from the other boxlike buildings in the area and have been built with, among other materials, gold.

North on Bay Street is the Canadian Imperial Bank of Commerce's perpetually 'chilly' complex of office buildings known as **Commerce Court**, designed by I.M. Pei. Across the street on the southwest corner is the **Toronto Dominion Centre** (66 Wellington Street), which almost single-handedly introduced the city to the international Modern Movement. Built originally with two towers, the building has gradually acquired more, with the total now at five. A popular spot among atmosphere-seeking diners is Canoe (*see page 77*), a fine restaurant situated on the 54th floor of the fourth tower.

The fifth tower actually hovers over the original Toronto Stock Exchange on Bay Street, now the **Design Exchange** (tel: 416-216-2140), a resource centre showcasing industrial design. Various lectures and exhibits are often open to the public.

Spreading out over the block on the northwest corner of King and Bay is **First Canadian Place**, and the adjacent **Exchange Tower**, which has housed the Toronto Stock Exchange since 1983. Within the tower is **Stock Market Place** (2 First Canadian Place, tel: 416-597-0965, Monday to Friday 10am–5pm; May to October also Saturday), a learning centre intended to demystify and enliven all aspects of the stock market.

Tour 3

Chinatown at Spadina Avenue

Chinatown, Kensington Market and the Art Gallery of Ontario (AGO)

Chinatown – Kensington Market – AGO – The Grange
See map on pages 14–15

27

A walk through Toronto's Chinatown and Kensington Market offers a glimpse at the ethnic enclaves that add a sumptuous texture to the city's urban weave.

The building of the New City Hall in 1959 swallowed a sizeable section of Chinatown, forcing it to move to the more westerly location it now encompasses. **Chinatown** has been described as geographically 'hyphenated', as it spans from Dundas Street West (from Bay to University) and from Beverly Street to Spadina. Exploring these streets reveals one of the city's bizarre contradictions: a cornucopia of bustling market activity fringing on the odd backdrop of ultra-modern downtown skyscrapers.

Out shopping

A vibrant mesh of colour, fetid odour and various Asian banter fills the streets of Toronto's Chinatown. This city within a city has grown to become one of the largest Chinatowns in North America, a reflection of Toronto's burgeoning ethnic Chinese population.

Canada saw its first Chinese settlers as a result of the gold rushes of the 1850s and 1860s. Later, the building of the Canadian Pacific Railway brought over 17,000 Chinese workers, who settled all over the country (one of the reasons most major cities have at least a small Chinatown). Toronto's Chinese community originated in the area along York Street between King and Queen Streets, a space now ensconced by towers of glass and metal. Remnants of the old Chinatown are still visible on Dundas Street West between Bay Street and University Avenue which developed out of the many restaurants, laundries and tea shops that cropped up between 1910 and the 1920s.

With freer immigration laws from the Liberal government in the 1960s, Toronto saw an influx of Asian newcomers from various areas of east and southeast Asia. Political instability in many southeast Asian countries and the uncertain future of Hong Kong were catalysts for many people seeking a new life in a foreign country where Asian roots were already established. To these people, Chinatown became more than grocery stores and curio shops; it was a meeting place and hub of Asian culture. It was also somewhere to find work and learn how to speak English while still enjoying the comfort of an Asian environment.

Walking up **Spadina Avenue** from Dundas Street West is a good introduction to the look, feel and smell of Toronto's Chinatown. Food is like a religion in China, so it is no wonder that the stalls flanking Spadina are laden with fresh fruit, vegetables, spices, meats and other culinary essentials – many unidentifiable even to the unrefined eye. Vegetables are particularly important and are found spilling out of almost every storefront. A diverse range of leafy greens, bamboo shoots, water chestnuts, taro and lotus roots punctuate the streetside stalls. Many stalls are also devoted to fruit. Spiky red rambutans, bright yellow star fruit, the infamously pungent durian, and the melt-in-your-mouth sweetness of a jack fruit can all be found here. There is an art to choosing the perfect fruit – just watch the time taken to tap, roll and smell an in-season durian to ensure a delectable choice. Barbecued pork and chicken also crowd the windowed shopfronts, and the scents of fresh and saltwater fish waft around you.

Durian fruit and other essentials

Restaurants have long been the mainstay of the area. Over the years the cuisine has taken its cues from the increasing diversity of the Asian immigrants, coupled with the public's growing palate for international fare. Instead of the old standby chop suey restaurants, Chinatown now offers a truer representation of China's regional cuisines: Cantonese, Sichuan, Huaiugan, not to mention the influx of influences from other places such as Singapore, Hong Kong, Malaysia, Vietnam.

Dim sum is a popular choice. Restaurants that specialise in it are jam-packed during the lunch hour, including **Kowloon** (5 Baldwin Street, tel: 416-977-3773), just off of Spadina, north of Dundas Street West.

No Chinese area would be complete without a wide array of herbal samplings. The hundreds of scents emanating from jars and bins full of dried plants, seeds, animal parts, minerals and roots can either repel or entice a curious browser. But for the plant lover there is certainly no shortage of herbal stops in the district.

Reflecting the economic growth of Toronto's Chinese enclave, shopping malls have begun to sprout up among the canopied stalls. Within these centres are Chinese stores selling everything from silk goods, to jade jewellery, to rice cookers. **Chinatown Centre** (222 Spadina Avenue, tel: 416-340-9367) is downtown Chinatown's biggest complex with over 100 stores. Further north and of the same ilk is the **Dragon City Complex** (280 Spadina Avenue, tel: 416-979-7777), which caters for a slightly more élite crowd and houses an excellent food complex in the centre court.

Dragon City clientele

Turning west on to St Andrew from Spadina, you will see a small stall-lined street linking Chinatown to another of Toronto's ethnic gems, **Kensington Market**. Kensington is a bit of an anomaly – an area where street names from Britain, foods from the Middle East to the Caribbean and vintage clothes of every era all try to eke out a harmonious existence. The market has a long history as a mercantile menagerie, and it very much retains this character today.

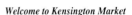

Welcome to Kensington Market

Known as The Jewish Market in the 1920s, it was established when Jewish pedlars, ostracised from the existing business community, began hawking their goods from pushcarts. Gradually they took over the houses in the area, converting them into stores. But the old tradition of displaying fruit, chickens and racks of clothing on the sidewalks remained.

An African community also existed alongside the Jewish immigrants. In fact, the popular Real Peking Restaurant (355 College Street) was originally the home of the Universal Negro Improvement Association in the 1930s. It was also a neighbourhood where black musicians performing in Toronto, including Sammy Davis Jr, could

Street art

Kensington Avenue

Fashion and food

find a friendly family to stay with at a time when the hotels wouldn't rent them rooms.

The ethnic face has since changed, but the same bustling atmosphere lives on. The area's residents have predominantly been immigrants who initially sought jobs in the Fashion District, found in the now mostly Chinese Spadina area. The Jewish community was slowly replaced by Portuguese West Indian, Chinese, Hungarian and Filipino merchants. The crowded houses, often in disrepair, were enlivened by Portuguese paint jobs: chartreuse with lavender and violet, alongside crimson and yellow, or aquamarine and orange-painted trims and boards. Kensington was the picture of ethnic Canada that Pierre Elliot Trudeau chose to use, in 1974, as the backdrop in a television commercial campaign.

Kensington Avenue south of St Andrew Street is lined with vintage clothing stores displaying their wares on the sidewalks. Individual shops come and go, but some manage staying power. **Courage My Love** (14 Kensington Avenue, tel: 416-979-1992) has been around for a while and offers an eclectic range of East Asian clothing, along with vintage items including hats, sweaters and crinoline dresses, and a large selection of beads, pendants and silver for making your own jewellery.

A walk westward from the corner of Kensington and Dundas leads up **Augusta Avenue**, another strip on the more culinary side of the market. Here the stores sell fresh fruit and vegetables, baked goods, meat and imported cheeses. Shops are not restricted to food, though. It is possible to find dry goods, furniture, electronics, clothes and just about anything else the shopkeepers feel like putting out that day. There are also many restaurants dotting the area, with choices ranging from small cafés to Portuguese and Laotian eateries.

A walk eastwards along Nassau Street and then south on Spadina until Dundas Street West leads back into the throes of Chinatown. Amid the Chinese restaurants and shops is Toronto's acclaimed gallery, the ★★★ **Art Gallery of Ontario (AGO)** (317 Dundas Street West, tel: 416-979-6648, Wednesday to Friday noon–9pm, Saturday and Sunday 10am–5.30pm). British artist Henry Moore's *Two Forms* are the draw for many visitors, befitting a gallery that contains the world's largest collection of his work – over 800 pieces.

The eighth-largest art museum in North America, the AGO houses over 24,000 works spanning a millennium of European, Canadian, modern and contemporary art. Although it displays the paintings of some world-famous artists such as Rembrandt, Degas, Dürer, Fragonard, Picasso, Gauguin, Brancusi and Rothco, the gallery is a

beneficial stop for those who are interested in learning more about Canadian art.

Outside the AGO

There is also a large collection of Inuit prints and sculpture, lending insight into the art of northern Canada's indigenous peoples. The impressive selection of pieces by Canadians creating in the European tradition spans the entire 20th century and represents a rich variety of artistic talent. From the stark hyper-realism of Nova Scotia's Alex Colville, to Emily Carr's West Coast-inspired works, the gallery offers a smattering of Canada's notables. Ontario's Group of Seven – a group of artists formed in 1912 who were masters of capturing the Canadian wilderness – provide a large body of work. Included in their paintings dating from the 1920s is a number of small panels or 'painted sketches' that evoke the energy and sense of immediacy that come from having been painted out in the wilds.

In addition to its permanent exhibits, the AGO hosts special one-offs. On occasion it curates some blockbuster exhibits which require tickets in advance and patience from viewers, who are often packed in tightly.

The gallery also offers educational programmes for adults and hands-on art classes for children, as well as film viewings. Its gift shop stocks a good variety of art books, including a wide selection on Canadian art and artists.

The Grange

The AGO was first housed in the **Grange** (Dudas Street West at Beverly Street behind the gallery), Toronto's oldest surviving brick house once owned by the Boulton family. Built in 1817, the Georgian house is linked to the museum by the opulent glassed-in Joey and Toby Tanenbaum Sculpture Atrium.

The adjacent **Grange Park** is now a public city park that had many defenders when plans to expand the AGO were to encroach upon it.

The Queen Street crowd

Tour 4

Queen Street West

Take your pick

Queen Street West (from Tecumseth Street to University Avenue) – Felician Sisters' Convent – City TV – Campbell House *See map on pages 14–15*

Every city has an area that attracts creativity, celebrates individuality and does it with panache. **Queen Street West** is one of these places. For over 20 years this street has been synonymous with the ever-intriguing grunge chic of the alternative crowd. A funky strip of shops, cafés and bars, it is home to fashion, art, poetry and punk, and to the people who create it.

Once between Peter and Simcoe Streets, the true face of this alternative district has shifted further west, fleeing the encroachment of the suits and high rents that have recently come to get their piece of the scene. To gain a feel for the area, take the Queen streetcar as far west as you feel like exploring (at least to Stanley Park at Queen and Walnut Avenue) and then head back eastwards, winding slowly along either side of the street.

Over two decades ago, Queen Street was a mess of old warehouses, abandoned sweat shops and deserted sidewalks. At night prostitutes and addicts would surface, etching out the subversive image. Slowly artists, writers, actors and musicians began to discover that the area offered a cheap way of life, with huge inexpensive lofts and catchpenny eateries. The art scene seemed to create itself spontaneously and began evolving to its own mythologies, despite being largely ignored by mainstream media. A wave of cultural nationalism punctuated the scene, and suddenly artists found themselves in a completely unscripted position: an era wedged between the mimicry of colonial culture and the current climate of all things American. Anything was possible.

The community began to spill along Queen towards the exotic whimsy of **Spadina Avenue**, where the constructs of art-friendly environs were well in place – diners, sidewalk stalls, bars, shady trees, high-ceilinged warehouses, dealers, secondhand wares and all-night stores. Raw street life was suddenly making its presence known to the prudish 'Toronto the good'. Surrounding immigrant neighbourhoods also helped to enrich the area with their varied cultures, ancient arts and linguistic nuances – all tied to the poetic dream of living in a free city.

Pronounced dead on numerous occasions, Queen Street has resisted every time, bouncing back with the resilience of a New York cockroach. Granted, the area has had to do the sidestep to avoid the tour buses, raised rents and mega chain stores, but somehow it has been able to retain the ferocious funk and vigour of its early days. It was, after all, built from cosmopolitan anarchy and the long, 12-hour days of multilingual residents. Even though Gap, Club Monaco and La Cache have shuffled the one-of-a-kind merchants westwards, to some the neighbourhood still 'looks like an old village tucked into the mountains of bank towers'.

A place for pool and beer

Starting from the westward end, there is the luring hand-painted sign of the **Gypsy Co-op** (at number 817), a pool hall and beer parlour with good food. Further east is the modest – but jam-packed with Aussie workboots – **Australian Boot Company** (at number 791). For those looking for footwear that combines function and fashion, the store is rife with the utilitarian chic found in a sea of lace-less boots.

Queen Street is flanked on both sides by boutiques and clothing stores, many of which are run by local designers. **J. Alfred Prufrock** (at number 652) and **Comrags** (at number 654) both offer upscale but very wearable clothing. **Romni Wools** (at number 658 on the north side of the street) is a mainstay for the knitting community and is spared the usual grandmother/spinster feel of most wool shops. It has to, considering it has survived so long in Toronto's edgiest neighbourhood.

Feet first

Evidence of the immigrant Polish, Ukrainian, Czech, Russian and Slavic Jew residents of the area appears when walking eastwards. The street becomes speckled with delicatessens of European flavour, with giveaway names such as Europe or Prague Deli. There are smells of sharp cheeses, fresh meats, pickled spices, breads and other European fare. The delis are separated by stores selling everything from used books to antiques. **Metro**, an

Metro for 'retro'

For live bands

innocuous little store on the south side of the street, is a blast from the past, brimming with 'retro' housewares. Browse and you can find *circa* 1960s' silver toasters, psychedelic rotary phones, lava lamps, records and just about anything you thought you would never see survive into the millennium.

At the corner of Bathurst and Queen is a black and purple building, in which live bands can be seen virtually any night of the week at **The Big Bop** and **The Reverb**. For concert listings and times, it is best to peruse one of Toronto's weekly entertainment papers, such as *Now* or *Eye*.

Strolling eastwards along Queen, **Pre-loved** (at number 611) is a boutique that offers an innovative blend of vintage and newly designed (or in some cases revamped) clothing. This section of Queen also caters for vinyl faithfuls with a clutch of secondhand record shops.

Among several Art Deco and antique shops is **Abelard Books** (at number 519, tel: 416-504-2665, Monday to Saturday 11–6pm, Sunday noon–5pm). Established in 1977 just west of Spadina, this bookstore is full of used, rare and early printed books. Specialising in philosophy, Greek and Latin classics, and medieval literature, it is a standout for those who enjoy the thrill of finding a unique literary treasure, or simply a good read.

Felican Sisters' Convent

A variety of fabric shops begin to edge out other stores in this section of Queen, largely a mix of the spill-over of Spadina's Fashion District and the boutique/clothing design shops indigenous to Queen Street. Of especial note is **Mokuba**, at the corner with Portland Street, for its amazing selection of ribbons and trim.

Between Bathurst and Spadina there are also a number of good, moderately priced eateries, including the **Vienna Café** (at number 626), with homemade granola and a fabulous eggs Bombay (a curried version of eggs Benedict) on the weekend breakfast menu.

Slightly north of Queen on Augusta is the **Felician Sisters' Convent** 🅑 (25 Augusta Avenue), the quintessential Victorian house. Replete with bonnet dormers, canopied windows and a gabled tower, it was built in 1876 for a dealer in 'Wools, Hides, Skins & Tallow'. Edward Leadly had a warehouse on Front Street but his 'sheepskin-pulling' factory was originally on this site. The building had a brief stint as a Salvation Army headquarters, but has served an order of nuns, who came to Toronto to work with the Polish immigrant community, since 1938.

A world apart from nuns and convents is the club scene, which filters through this area too. Pioneer of the original Queen Street action, **The Cameron House** (408 Queen

The Cameron House

Street West) was once the epicentre. An ardent supporter of art, this constantly buzzing tavern nurtured young talent by commissioning them to exhibit their works on its walls. Now 3-D bugs over 60cm (2ft) long can be seen crawling up the sides of the old building.

The Zoo Bar West, the Bovine Sex Club and Savage Garden also stake out their position in the nightclub scene along Queen Street West.

At Spadina, Chinatown meets the Fashion District and once again fabric and notion shops abound. East of Spadina leads into the original site of Queen West, although now it has a more slick and upscale urban feel than its early days as bohemian mecca. There are some great eating spots here, though they are a little pricier than their more westward counterparts. **Peter Pan** (aptly on Queen at the corner of Peter Street) and the **Queen Mother Café** (208 Queen Street West) are long-established and excellent eateries. The **Bamboo** (at number 312, *see page 80*) is also a longtime resident of the area and, with a rooftop terrace, tasty Thai/Caribbean dishes and live music, it remains popular – especially in summer. Another old-timer is the legendary **Horseshoe Tavern** (at number 368, *see page 81*), a raunchy, draught-drinking place to see great live music.

Bamboo with a view

35

To experience one of Toronto's oldest inns (so they say), try the **Black Bull Tavern** close to Soho Street on Queen. Parts of it supposedly date back to 1833 when Toronto was still the muddy-streeted town of York.

Drinks at the Black Bull

Between Duncan and John Streets is the original home of The Methodist Book and Publishing Company, later known as the Ryerson Press. The building now houses Moses Znaimer's ★ **City TV** ⓰. For a dollar you can spout off at the camera and possibly catch yourself later on the station's programme, *Speaker's Corner*.

Also fitting for this area is the Word on The Street Festival, an outdoor book fair held each fall, featuring readings, books for sale and events for children.

One block west of University Avenue at Simcoe Street marks the end of the Queen Street scene as skyscrapers and tall office towers of downtown now come into full view. Oddly sandwiched between the two worlds is ★★ **Campbell House** ⓱ (160 Queen Street West, tel: 416-597-0227, Monday to Friday 9.30am–4.30pm). This *circa* 1822 building is the earliest surviving example of Georgian architecture from the time when Toronto was the town of York, and was home to William Campbell, the first Canadian judge to be knighted. The house has been renovated and partially restored to serve as the home of the Law Society of Upper Canada, the trade union of Ontario's legal profession, and is open for tours.

Campbell House

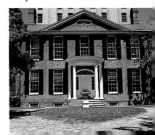

University flag on
Ontario Avenue

Tour 5

Queens Park, University of Toronto and Museums

Ontario Legislative Building – University of Toronto
– Royal Ontario Museum – Museum of Ceramic Art
– Bata Shoe Museum *See map on pages 14–15*

Perhaps the true lifeblood of the city, Queens Park and the sprawling campus of the University of Toronto together serve as a reminder of the elegant architecture and pastoral setting of this place's early days. Politics, academia and culture breathe life into the area's stately buildings and bucolic enclaves.

Legislative detail

The **Ontario Legislative Building** ⑱ (University Avenue north of College Street, tel: 416-325-7500, Monday to Friday 9am–6pm) was built in the Richardson Romanesque style that was popularised in the 19th century to a design by Richard A. Waite. Waite caused a scandal when the inflated price tag of his creation far surpassed what had originally been agreed. The building is home to the legislative assembly, and when the House is sitting the public is welcome to observe in the visitors' gallery. Tours are also available and it is advisable to call ahead for schedule information as times are subject to change. (A rather ironic footnote is the fact that this, the seat of the Ontario government, resides in a building where a mental institution once sat.)

Just west of Queens Park and University Avenue is the sprawling **University of Toronto** (U of T) campus. Slap bang in the middle of the city, the campus not only houses an eclectic bunch of buildings, it also retains the green stretches that added to its once-rural setting. From

Queens Park, King's College Circle is a quick sideward jaunt west and a transition from 19th-century splendour to Gothic-esque stature.

The university began with a royal charter endowed by the members of the Church of England, and a parcel of 65 hectares (160 acres). Many Torontonians did not want this government-funded institution to be Anglican, resulting in an act in 1849 that declared it to be non-denominational – which was a rather radical stance in the era of church affiliation.

Although originally visually cohesive, a fire swept through the campus in 1890 and the subsequent rebuilding and constant expansion led the university to look like the architectural hodgepodge it is today. Some styles are good, some downright bad.

For those who wish to experience the full campus atmosphere, it is possible to book a room in one of the many residences that offer accommodation from early May to late August. The numbers can be obtained from the campus housing service (tel: 416-978-8045) as each residence must be contacted separately. For academia-philes there are tours available (tel: 416-978-4111). Or, for those who wish to soak up the academic and historic atmosphere, a casual stroll around campus can be inspiring.

★★★ **University College** ⓲ (15 King's College Circle), a disjointed blend of Romanesque, medieval, Gothic and classical, has always been an anomaly. The building attracts visitors and students alike, as it exudes the grace and ennoblement of higher learning – a true embodiment of collegiate life.

Just north of King's College Circle is the Hart House Circle, home of the **Hart House** (7 Hart House Circle). A gift from farm-machinery magnate Hart Massey, the building was designed in a late-Gothic revival style that had long been associated with ancient places of learning. Although intended as a male undergraduate centre, it now serves the whole academic community. Encircling the quadrangle used for outdoor summer concerts, the building houses a gym, a pool, activity rooms, lecture rooms, a chapel, a small theatre and a restaurant.

Backtracking in the direction you came, to the southwest of King's College Circle, **Knox College** (extending from 59 St George Street through to 23 King's College Circle) is so much the image of hallowed halls of academia that it has been chosen as the backdrop for several movies, including *The Paper Chase*, *Moonstruck* and *Dead Ringers*.

Along with the Gothic, medieval and classical structures of the campus, there is also a string of modern buildings worth exploring. A couple of blocks north of Knox College lies **Massey College** (4 Devonshire Place).

Graduation day

37

Lunch outside Hart House

College entrance detail

Conceived by Vincent Massey (also of farm-machinery fame), the building served as a centre for male graduates upon opening in 1963, only to become co-ed in the mid-1970s. The college's fame stems from the notoriety of a previous longtime principal, the grand old man of Canadian letters, Robertson Davies.

Innis College (2 Sussex Avenue) dispels the myth of pomposity equated with higher learning. Its subtle, unpretentious structure seeks to mesh with its environment rather than coolly stand back from it.

Two streets west of Sussex Avenue and situated appropriately close to Philosopher's Walk, is the Romantic-fashioned **Trinity College** (6 Hoskin Avenue). Built on Queen Street in 1851, it was replicated in 1925 at the current location. A feel of England's ivied halls echoes from this building, which borrowed its Tudor Gothic accents from Oxford and Cambridge Universities.

Royal Ontario Museum

A stroll up Philosopher's Walk, a small, winding pathway, seemingly designed to induce thought, leads to the ★★★ **Royal Ontario Museum** ❷⓿ (along Bloor Street West to Queens Park Avenue, tel: 416-586-8000, Monday 10am–6pm, Tuesday 10am–8pm, Wednesday to Saturday 10am–6pm, Sunday 11am–6pm). Now run by the provincial government, the ROM enjoys the illustrious position of being one of the largest museums in North America. With its Venetian Byzantine details, arched windows and buff-coloured brick, the facade of the building viewed from Philosopher's Walk is one of subtle grandeur. The first addition to the original design in 1830 fashioned the museum into an H-shape which has since been filled in by subsequent expansion.

Housed within its walls, on four different levels, is an expansive collection that touches upon a mélange of realms. From the vast Life Sciences collection to ancient artefacts from all corners of the world, the sheer volume and scope of the holdings is impressive.

Found on the street level of the gallery is the rich Asian collection. The museum is arguably best known for its extensive Chinese exhibits which were largely gathered in the first third of this century. The majority of the items were collected by George Crofts whose fur-trading exploits at the turn of the century led him to China, which in the 1920s was going through a turbulent transition period. This unique position allowed Crofts to acquire impressive pieces: from the Ming temple replete with tomb sculptures, stone arches and, remarkably, a set of stone figures that once stood on the very avenue that led to the burial plot, to the Imperial wardrobe.

The Bishop White Gallery of Chinese Temple Art showcases impressive Buddhist sculptures, surrounded by

Sculpture of Zu Dashou (above) and the Ming temple (below)

Buddha sculpture

mammoth paintings of Buddhist and Taoist gods from the 13th century. Within the collection there are also exquisite perfume bottles, delicate bowls, intricate carvings of jade and ivory and hundreds of other fine *objets d'art*.

It stands to reason that a Canadian museum should be rich in the art and artefacts of its own country, and the Royal Ontario Museum is no exception. For a look at this heritage, Ontario archaeology and the nation's indigenous peoples, the floor below the main level offers a broad sweep of things Canadian. The Naskapi of Labrador, the Iroquois and Ojibway of Ontario and their predecessors, the Plains indigenous peoples, the Innuit of the far north and the spectacular art of the various northwest coast tribes are all represented. There is also one gallery dedicated to Canada's Peoples Exhibitions, which features changing exhibits spanning from past to present on a wide variety of topics.

The energetic Life Sciences collection can be found on the second level. Though a popular stop for kids, it is fascinating for old and young alike. Dinosaur skeletons appear in what seems to be their natural habitat, a gallery is dedicated to evolution, and there are informative displays of mammals, birds, insects and reptiles. This level also houses of the popular bat cave, an exact copy of St Clair cave found in Jamaica. Not for the squeamish, it enables visitors to walk through and experience the sights and sounds of a true-to-life bat cave, complete with over 2,500 simulated bats.

Level three plays host to extensive Mediterranean holdings. Starting with Romanesque art, the collection predominately displays decorative arts including pottery, glass and English furniture. Sculpture of all periods is represented, along with fine ivories, silver and bronzes. There is also an interesting print collection and a large array of

Totem pole

39

Dinosaur remains

Newly knighted

arms and armour that extends beyond Europe, with Japanese and Islamic exhibits and a collection of Indo-Persian weapons to peruse.

Other exhibitions of note are the European musical instruments and the textile collection. The musical instruments date back as far as the 16th century and can be heard with the help of the high-tech sound system. ROM's textile collection is ranked fifth in importance in the world and features textiles and costumes from every period and every part of the world.

All of the museum's work is based on research and teaching – both formal and informal – so it is no wonder that learning plays an integral role in the activities. On the second floor, the Discovery Gallery allows everyone over seven years old to get their hands on objects from the collections and to view them with microscopes and magnifying glasses.

For those who would like to bring something home with them, the museum has four shops that feature everything from ROM's own publications to various other educational items and books, plus toys and gifts.

40

Museum of Ceramic Art

For a further look into the world of art and artefacts, the George R. Gardiner ★ **Museum of Ceramic Art** (111 Queen's Park, tel: 416-586-8080, Monday to Saturday 10am–5pm, Tuesday until 8pm, Sunday 11am–5pm) showcases an outstanding array of ceramics. The collection features objects from a myriad of cultures, dating from 3000BC to the 16th century. Observe ancient Mayan pottery, 16th-century Italian majolica pottery, puzzle jugs and posset pots from 17th-century England, and elegant scent bottles of the 18th century.

In The Clay Pit, would-be ceramic artists can learn from the pros as hands-on clay classes and other craft workshops are offered. The Gardiner Shop, with its array of Canadian ceramics and monthly shows of selected artists, is worth a visit.

Bata Shoe Museum:
Exhibits from Nigeria

North on Queens Park and a westward stroll along Bloor leads you to a new and funky addition to the museum scene: the ★★ **Bata Shoe Museum** ㉑ (327 Bloor Street West, tel: 416-979-7799, Tuesday, Wednesday, Friday and Saturday 10am–5pm, Thursday 10am–8pm, Sunday noon–5pm). Although a seemingly odd object to revere, this innovative collection offers a fascinating insight into culture, fashion and history from the vantage point of, what else – shoes. The curators will argue that history, politics and culture are directly rooted to footwear in this museum, which houses everything from 2,000-year-old Japanese *waraji* to a pair of black leather platforms that belonged to former Spice Girl Geri Halliwell.

Tour 6

Inside the Palm House

Cabbagetown

Allan Gardens – Palm House – Trinity Mews – Riverdale Park – Necropolis Cemetery and Chapel – Wellesley Park – Wellesley Cottages – Toronto Dance Theatre – St James' Cemetery and Chapel *See map on pages 14–15*

Rife with a past of gritty edginess, Cabbagetown has emerged to become one of Toronto's most historically rich neighbourhoods. Sprinkled with houses of cool brick, richly coloured and delicately etched glass windows and carved wood doors, the area is one of Toronto's oldest. A charming district to stroll and enjoy some of the most architecturally diverse dwellings in the city, it was once given the dubious distinction of being 'the largest Anglo-Saxon slum in North America' by local writer and now-famous Cabbagetown resident Morley Callahan.

A neighbourhood with history
Doorway detail

In the 1790s, when the Don River was full of salmon and surrounded by gooseberry bushes, Toronto's first lieutenant governor, John Graves Simcoe, built a modest cottage facetiously named Castle Frank. In the name of convenience, a road was laid to it from Lake Ontario. At the foot of the road, a couple of Toronto's first parliament buildings were built and eventually it became known as Parliament Street – a name that still holds today. Lined with everything from funky cafés and clothing stores to dry cleaners and laundrymats, Parliament Street cuts a swath through modern Cabbagetown and remains the major artery of the area.

The 'town' itself began to grow in the 1840s when, fleeing from the potato famines in their homeland, thousands of Irish immigrants settled in the area east of Parliament

'Victorian' heritage

Allan Gardens and the Palm House

Street in workers' cottages. Because times were tough, vegetables, including cabbages, were planted in every available space. The front lawns lined with cabbages resulted in the Cabbagetown moniker, which has stuck through the decades. Due to its overwhelming number of Northern Irish residents, the area also came to be known as 'Little Belfast'.

In the 1930s, the Depression hit hard and the houses fell into disrepair. During a period of urban renewal in the 1950s, much of the area south of Gerrard was demolished. But it took a couple more decades before Cabbagetown's potential as a distinctive residential district close to the heart of the city started to spark an interest. Houses began to return to being single-family dwellings after being divided into very small apartments following the World War II population boom. With these homes newly restored to their original splendour, Cabbagetown contained, according to the *New York Times*, 'the largest collection of Victorian homes in North America'.

Although not in Old Cabbagetown, ★★ **Allan Gardens** (Sherbourne and Carlton Streets, tel: 416-392-7288) sits on the edge of the 'town' at Sherbourne and Carlton Streets. An exotic and bucolic reminder of the green spaces that were once a hallmark of the area, the park is the result of a donation by George William, the son of wealthy merchant William Allan, who bequeathed the land to the city to be used for horticultural gardens. Opened officially in 1860 by the Prince of Wales, the gardens took on an air of pomp and grandeur. The building of the glittering Crystal Palace in 1878 set the stage for opulent events, including when an unknown 25-year-old charismatic writer by the name of Oscar Wilde came to speak to sold-out houses in the summer of 1882. Before being destroyed by a fire in 1902, the pavilion had been the only large concert hall in use in Toronto.

Smack in the middle of the gardens is the **Palm House,** a lavish glass dome connected to six greenhouses. Delicate green leaves and lusciously coloured flowers snake and curve their way around the sunny glass walls. There are hints of lush far-off places: Egyptian papyrus, pointsettias from Mexico, Japanese sweet flag and silver thatch palm from Trinidad. Free of charge and open to the public seven days a week, the Palm House provides a tranquil setting in which to collect thoughts, ponder or just relax amid the sweet fragrances.

A short walk eastwards along Carlton Street passes by the eclectic mix of housing that characteristically punctuates Cabbagetown. Roughcast cottages thrown in with Georgian, Gothic revival and Second Empire houses all line the street, some converted into offices and some very much lived in. It is here that some of the houses Oscar Wilde described as having 'horrid white brick' can be found, although some took his cue and have since been painted over.

South on Parliament at the corner of Spruce just west of Sackville Street lies the **Trinity Mews** (41 Spruce Street). A large, red-and-yellow brick building dating from 1859, Trinity Mews was part of Trinity College on Queen. After falling to a variety of owners over the years, it has finally been resurrected, with the neatly laid brick patterning the courtyard one of its best features.

43

Spruced up on Spruce Street

East of Sackville on the north side are the Spruce Court Apartments, the city's first government-sponsored housing project. Strolling north on Sumach and east along Geneva Street, the roads are flanked on either side by 'working-class cottages' built in the Alpha style.

This is also the site of historic ★★ **Riverdale Park** ㉓ (Carlton to Winchester Street). At one time the park encompassed 65 hectares (160 acres) on either side of the Don River; the great stands of gigantic red and white pine trees growing on the surrounding hills have since been diminished by the obtrusive Don Valley Parkway.

The City of Toronto originally bought this land for conversion into a park and industrial farm, and it remains an interesting outing for its terraced site and historic associations. In 1894, two wolves and a few deer prompted the beginnings of a zoological collection – to be known as Riverdale Zoo – that would last for over 80 years. Shuffling its animals to the newly opened Metro Toronto Zoo (now the Toronto Zoo, *see page 56*) in the late-1970s, the Riverdale Farm facility was transformed into a picturesque farmyard, replete with capacious 19th-century barns. Attempting to reclaim the original ecology of the

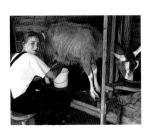

Riverdale farm hand

The Necropolis Chapel

area, two community planting events took place on the park's east side in 1991, and since then organisations and volunteers have planted over 6,000 native trees and shrubs.

Spearing the horizon north of the park is the eye-catching chapel, along with the gate and gatehouse, of the ★ **Necropolis Cemetery**. The cemetery dates back to the early 1850s when a group of concerned citizens banded together in search of a new site for the town's non-sectarian burying ground which at the time stood dangerously close to the burgeoning town of Yorkville. Literally meaning 'city of the dead', Necropolis rests on the ridge of the Don Valley, its pastoral grounds creating a mystic setting, not to mention the final resting place, of many notable Toronto pioneers including the city's first mayor, William Lyon Mackenzie. The adjacent **Necropolis Chapel** (200 Winchester Street) was built in 1872 in High Victorian Gothic style. With a web of vines clutching on to its outer brick walls and its striking stature, the chapel takes on an almost medieval feel.

Further up Sumach and east on Amelia Street along the edge of the Necropolis lies **Wellesley Park**. Continuing along on up to Wellesley and just past Sackville, there is a street sign for the ★ **Wellesley Cottages**. These quaint dwellings, once abundant, are now an architectural rarity. They have also been credited as being one of the only indigenous forms of Ontario architecture. Built in the 1870s as one-and-a-half storey labourers' cottages, these seven residences were the winning culmination of a design competition in England for a workman's cottage. The result is a little lane with a rural charm that manages to create a tiny enclave of tranquillity.

St James' Cemetery and chapel

Walk south on Sackville, then wander around the area through various sections of Sackville, Amelia, Metcalfe, Winchester and Carlton Streets. Cabbagetown's true architectural mixed-bag is evident in these roads laced with dwellings of Georgian, Gothic Revival and Second Empire elements. Standing at the corner of Winchester and Metcalfe is the **Toronto Dance Theatre** (80 Winchester, tel: 416-967-1365), which was originally constructed as a Romanesque church. Further south at 377 Sackville is the Shields House, which remains the only house in Toronto where the owner opted to build a stone front to cover the original brick.

Back on to Parliament Street, a stroll northwards leads to ★★ **St James' Cemetery** ㉔ and **St James the Lesser Chapel** (635 Parliament Street). With a 13th-century air about it, the chapel is often credited as being one of the most beautiful church buildings in Canada. The cemetery, like that of Necropolis, is the resting place for many of Toronto's well-established families.

Tour 7

Harbourfront and the Toronto Islands

Queen's Quay Terminal – Habourfront Centre –
Hanlan's Point – Toronto City Centre Airport –
Centreville – Algonquin Island – Ward's Island

One of the most popular things to do on a sunny summer
day in Toronto is to head for the cool waters and sun-
flecked skies of the waterfront. Ten minutes from downtown and on the shore of the lake, Harbourfront is saturated
with theatres, galleries, shops, studios and restaurants.
A 10-minute ferry ride to Centre Island offers a further
escape from the urbane – into the abundant gardens and
winsome charm of Toronto's islands.

Trapeze lessons at the
Harbourfront (below)

The Harbourfront area spans Queen's Quay between
Bathurst and York Streets. Originally 40 hectares (100
acres) of largely abandoned industrial land, it was transformed into Canada's first urban national park. After the
opening of the St Lawrence Seaway in 1959, planning was
centred around commercial use only. The area had grown
into a tangled web of industry that included shipping
facilities, warehouses, railway tracks, grain silos and
factories – all dotting, and obscuring, the shoreline. The

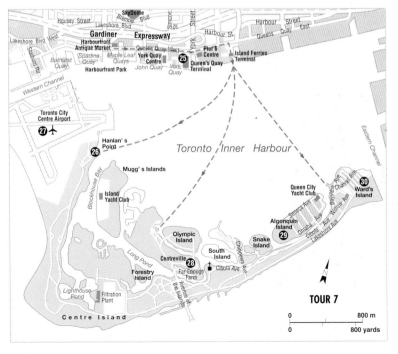

Queen's Quay Terminal

Harbourfront Centre and artisan

proposal to create Harbourfront offered a chance to reclaim the recreational aspect and link the city back to its estranged waterfront.

Now a 4-hectare (10-acre) complex of theatres, shops and galleries, Harbourfront is strategically poised between the lake and the foot of downtown. The area is a lively mix of residential, commercial and cultural activities. This is a place where co-ops and luxury condos stand side by side, where poetry festivals share the limelight with body-building competitions and canoe classes, and where antique vendors set up shop next to Art Deco boutiques.

The ★ **Queen's Quay Terminal** ㉕ (207 Queen's Quay West, tel: 416-203-0510), located at the foot of York Street, was one of the largest warehouses in North America when it opened in 1927. Renovated in 1981 to the chic centre of sophistication it is today, the complex houses over 100 shops, galleries and restaurants. Stores range from home and design boutiques, to shops with clothing, one-of-a-kind jewellery and Canadian crafts. There is a broad range of eateries in the Queen's Quay Terminal – from independent fast food, to mid-priced seaside bars to pricier establishments such as Chinese of Pink Pearl and the Westin Harbour Castle restaurants.

Part of the mandate proposed by Harbourfront's former general manager Howard Cohen was to oversee selling development rights to finance various cultural programmes – an agreement still in existence (although slightly waning) today. The ★★★ **Harbourfront Centre** (235 Queen's Quay West, tel: 416-973-4600), just steps away from the Queen's Quay Terminal, is brimming with contemporary culture. Here you can watch a play, find music and dance performances, and browse through galleries and craft studios. The centre is also the venue for literary readings, children's events and marine activities. The social, cultural and recreational hub of the neighbourhood, it hosts more than 4,000 diverse events every year, ranging from craft workshops and sailing lessons to jazz festivals and food fairs.

Among the major festivals held in the area is the annual mid-May Milk International Children's Festival, which presents dozens of performances by musicians, dancers, acrobats, actors, storytellers and magicians. In keeping with the cultural side of things, Harbourfront also hosts the prestigious International Author's Festival in the fall, along with offering weekly readings by authors from around the world almost every Tuesday evening.

The **Du Maurier Theatre Centre** (231 Queen's Quay West, tel: 416-973-3000) and the **York Quay Centre** (South side of Queen's Quay at York Street, tel: 416-973-4875) put on various theatrical presentations. Music can also be found in the York Quay Centre, with free concerts held on Sundays at the Du Maurier Theatre.

A further attraction is the **Harbourfront Antique Market** (390 Queen's Quay West, tel: 416-260-2626, Tuesday to Sunday 10am–6pm), which is Canada's largest antique market, featuring over 100 antique dealers and 30,769sq m (40,000sq ft) of antiques, with free admission and parking available. Flea and craft markets often surface in association with festivals and usually take place in Ann Tindal Park.

Inside the Antique Market

From Harbourfront you can see the outlying islands. Toronto was born of the water. The port has thrived and kept the city growing, but not without some considerable change. The **Toronto Islands** were originally a long, narrow peninsula jutting into Lake Ontario from the eastern part of the harbour, now called Cherry Beach. But in the 1850s a series of violent storms separated this peninsula from the mainland. The resulting archipelago of 18 variously sized islands rapidly grew into a popular summer retreat, complete with hotels, amusement parks and summer cottages.

47

Long before the islands became the playground for Toronto's élite, the Mississauga Indians were the first people to inhabit the area, when it was still a peninsula connected to mainland. It soon became popular with newly arrived English and French settlers, particularly with British officers and their wives as a spot to picnic, and with local farmers who saw the island's lush meadows as optimum grazing pastures for their cattle.

Abundant with ponds and lagoons, the islands were swarming with fish and game and became *the* spot for hunters and anglers, who built primitive cabins along its shores. The first large-scale residential use of the islands began in the 1870s, when Toronto's aristocracy built

Heading for the islands

En route to Hanlan's Point

Gibraltar Point Lighthouse

Colourful Centreville

elaborate Victorian-style cottages spanning from Hanlan's Point, through Centre Island, to the western edge of Ward's Island. **Hanlan's Point** 🟤 was the site of the first summer cottage community where as many as 40 dwellings dotted the West Island Drive. The area was named after Ned Hanlan, a renowned Canadian oarsman – who went on to set a world record in 1876 and win many world championships – and his family, who lived on the island and were among the first to settle there.

Today it is the locale of Hanlan's Point Ferry Terminal, which lies just southeast of the **Toronto City Centre Airport** 🟤. The area has some quiet spots tucked away on the westerly beaches, despite its proximity to the busy island airport. At the southernmost point is the **Gibraltar Point Lighthouse**. Built in 1808, it is the oldest structure on the islands that still stands on its original site.

The most popular summer destination of the islands are the lively, well-groomed grounds of **Centre Island**. When you arrive there, a flower-flanked esplanade leads directly to ★★★ **Centreville** 🟤 (16 May to 7 September, tel: 416-203-0405), an unassuming amusement park for children, designed to resemble a turn-of-the-century village complete with a petting zoo and plenty of animals. The park has over 30 rides and attractions including a ferris wheel, a beautiful antique carousel, a railroad station train ride, and paddle boats. There are dozens of fast-food outlets, but the setting is more conducive to a leisurely picnic for those inclined to plan ahead. The islands are all linked by small bridges, so to explore the whole lot, canoes and bikes can be rented nearby.

Life has been far from tranquil for the permanent residents throughout the past few decades. The islands were earmarked strictly for recreational use, with plans to evict and seize the homes of islanders. 'The city wants to tear down the houses,' author Margaret Atwood voiced through a character who lives on the island in her novel *Robber Bride*. '[She] sees it as envy: if the city people can't live here themselves they don't want anyone else to be able to do it either'. After a long, hard-fought battle with various levels of government and even a Supreme Court case, the islanders won the right to stay full-time residents after a 99-year lease was signed, finally securing their own future and that of their neighbourhood.

The communities of Wards and Algonquin islands make for an interesting stroll – a peek at the difference of an island life that is only minutes away from skyscrapers and traffic. There are actually no private cars on the island, leaving walking and cycling to maintain the rustic charm that has always lured both visitors and residents alike.

Cycling, jogging, canoeing – and in the winter cross-country skiing and skating on the lake – have all been a way of life since the beginning of these communities, and continues to be so today.

Despite the umbrella of island life, there are distinct differences between the island communities. ★ **Algonquin Island** ㉙ was built in the 1940s on suburban-sized lots, so people there tend to stay on their own property and visit each other in a similar manner to suburbanites. ★ **Ward's Island** ㉚, on the other hand, began in the 19th century as a tent city, with houses crowded together, breeding an exceedingly close-knit community. However, both communities purport a level of trust among neighbours that seems to be a throwback to earlier generations found on the mainland. Another example of this closeness is the way that people combine their gardens – behind the houses on Ward's Island it isn't surprising to find a communal garden, where a few tiny cottages have developed their grounds together creating a park-like feel. The houses of the two communities have mostly wood exteriors ensconced in a rustic setting that evokes the charm of a picture postcard. The communities also offer a glimpse of the past, and a different way of life, which exists in sharp contrast to their high-powered urban backdrop.

Ward Island cottages

To get to the islands, proceed to the ferry docks that lie just behind the Westin Harbour Castle. The schedules change according to season. In the summer months (24 May to 7 September), the ferries run from 8am to 11.45pm and there is regular service every 30 minutes, or every 15 minutes during peak hours. In the spring, fall and winter, they run to Hanlan's Point and Ward's Island only. It's advisable to call ahead during the off-seasons as times vary and are subject to change without notice (tel: 416-392-8193).

A driftwood fence

Discovering the beaches

Tour 8

The Beaches

50

Speeding on the Martin Goodman Trail

Steps to the shore

R.C. Harris Water Filtration Plant – Victoria Park – Balmy Beach – Boardwalk – Martin Goodman Trail – Kew Beach Park – Kew Gardens – Queen Street East shopping and eateries

Only 15 minutes from downtown, the distinctly lackadaisical community of 'the Beaches' (also referred to as 'the Beach') is rife with possibility. From recreational pursuits for the actively inclined, to strolling through the shop-lined streets or eating at an outdoor café, it offers a breezy alternative to the fast pace of the city.

A little more than a century ago, this area was designated cottage country for Toronto's élite. The geographical location – separated from the city by the Don River and situated right on the shore of Lake Ontario – prompted the label of resort community from the beginning. Even when it became a part of Toronto it managed to retain its separate identity, and continues to do so today.

The area was first settled in as early as 1793, at which time the beach and its environs where divided into lots. The resort community began as cottagey clapboard houses along the lake shore complete with amusement grounds, canoe clubs and hotels. A road was built eastward (later to be known as **Kingston Road**, *see* backcover map) and along it clusters of buildings, taverns, a school and a steam saw-mill sprouted up. In the latter half of the 1800s, large parcels of land were set aside for parks – a legacy still much enjoyed today.

By the 1870s, the area was served by a streetcar and a steamer and had developed as a summer retreat. Victoria

Park opened in 1878 and Kew Gardens the following year. People began to flock to the parks, many of them living in cottages for a period in the summer. The cottages soon became winterised into permanent homes and visitors kept pouring in. Woodbine, Kew Gardens, Scarboro, Balmy Beach and Victoria Park collectively became Toronto's playgrounds by the lake. The city of Toronto began to expand eastward, and by the 1920s the Beaches was subdivided for year-round residential development.

A place to unwind…

The Beaches remains one of Toronto's most popular areas for tourists to explore. To begin, take the Queen streetcar to Neville Park Boulevard. From here you can stroll down to Nursewood Road, where the ★★★ **R.C. Harris Water Filtration Plant** ❸ (2701 Queen Street East at Victoria Avenue, tel: 416-392-3566, drop-in tours 10am, 11.30am, 1pm on Saturday only) austerely makes itself known. Although it sounds mundane, the building is an elegant structure perched on a spectacular locale. Apparently ad and movie execs think so too – the place is usually crawling with crews shooting commercials, television or movie scenes, so it is best to call ahead if you want to take a tour. The plant also garnered attention from world-renowned Toronto author Michael Ondaatje in his novel *In the Skin of a Lion*; in defence of building such an overtly opulent structure during the Depression, he wrote, "'The form of a city changes faster than the heart of a mortal,' Harris liked to remind his critics, quoting Baudelaire'.

…and purify

The plant sits on what were formerly amusement parks from the Beaches' early days. Built in the 1930s, it is bedecked with rose-coloured marble floors, tiles from

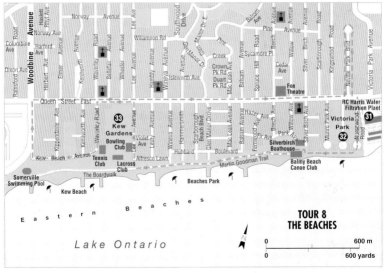

**TOUR 8
THE BEACHES**

Lake Ontario

0   600 m
0   600 yards

Inside the plant

Sienna and funky Art Deco clocks. There are also marble walls and copper-banded roofs, with the entrance modelled from a Byzantine city gate.

Function does proceed over form, however, as this is the site where water is cleaned for millions. The edge of the property offers a stunning vantage point from which to see the magnanimity of the lake – its sapphire waters crashing below.

From the plant you can follow the Nursewood Road to its dead-end and then continue westward towards **Victoria Park** ❷ (sprawling between Nursewood Road and the Boardwalk along the water). Although some remnants of the former parks remain, there is little to represent how popular and widely used they were in their former glory. West of Victoria Park is where Munro Amusement Park, built by the street railway company, used to be.

At this point the **Boardwalk** is visible, hugging the shore and very much giving the waterfront the look and feel of a lakeside resort town. A solidly built path of springy wooden planks, this is a popular walk for both Torontonians and tourists, and is probably the most famous landmark of the area. Skirted by the ★ **Martin Goodman Trail** (a path that now runs the length of Toronto's waterfront for 325km/202 miles), the Boardwalk spans the city's waterfront from the Beaches to the Humber River and is pleasant for a stroll year round.

Next to Victoria Park and along the Boardwalk is **Balmy Beach**. Originally a gift given by a former mayor to the Town of East Toronto, it is also home of the Balmy Beach Canoe Club, made famous by Roy Nurse, who brought home three gold medals from the 1924 Paris Olympics. The club, a community institution since 1905, is today a popular spot to play beach volleyball. Further along the shorefront was the location of the Scarboro Beach Amusement Park, which was purported to be the largest and busiest park during its heyday (1907–25).

Balmy Beach

Kew Gardens

The last of the notables in the Beaches and still standing today is ★★ **Kew Gardens** ❸ (2075 Queen Street East at Lee Avenue). This was formerly a farm, but in 1879 its owner, Joseph Williams, made it into a private park and named it after the famous botanical gardens in London, England. His son, whom he also named Kew, built an impressive stone house at the foot of Lee Avenue in 1902. When the city expropriated the land in 1907, the house was all he was left with.

Kew Garden's languid gazebo has been the social centre of the area for some time, as it hosts many annual events, including the Christmas Tree and Menorah Lighting Festival, a jazz festival in the summer, and an arts

and crafts show. The 1920 wooden **Leuty Lifeguard Station**, recently restored, is still functioning today.

After enjoying the waterfront, walk northward from Kew Gardens up to Queen Street East where it intersects Woodbine Avenue. Along the way is a chance to peruse the large variety of architectural house styles on the tree-lined streets that wind their way towards the lake. Many of the original beach cottages built in the latter half of the 1800s and early-1900s have been modernised and are still standing today, although the majority of the Beaches' permanent homes sprang up during the 1920s and 1930s.

Leuty Lifeguard Station

Queen Street East is the most commercial of the Beaches' shopping districts, but also the most plentiful in terms of shops, boutiques, restaurants and cafés. This stretch is steeped with colourful storefronts emanating the beach motif that caters for the tourist trade. The area is also very family-oriented, flanked with kids' clothing and toy stores, candy and chocolate shops, and tempting ice-cream parlours. The coffee giants have descended too, with a Starbucks on practically every corner, as well as Second Cup, Grabba Jabba and other home-grown coffee shops speckling the street. A warm breezy day, however, is highly conducive to spreading out on one of the outdoor patios and sipping a frothy coffee while people-watching or reading the paper.

Jessie's Gate on Queen Street East

You can find just about anything along Queen Street East, including the olfactory seduction of **Lush** (at number 2014), a British bath shop with windows piled high with chunky homemade wheels of soap and rose petal-stuffed bath 'bombs'. There are also countless shoe stores, natural food shops, used and new bookstores, clothes boutiques and a jangle of restaurants of equal, middle-of-the-road calibre.

Beachy House wares

Black Creek Pioneer Village:
a stroll into the past

Meet the knitters and weavers

Further Sights

Away from the central areas of interest in Toronto there are a wide range of alluring spots to explore. From the seasonal but long historical tradition of the Canadian National Exhibition (CNE) to the opulence of Toronto's only castle, there is no shortage of sights that stand alone but are well worth a special trip. The following are listed alphabetically and deserve a visit if time permits.

★★ **Black Creek Pioneer Village** in northwest Toronto (1000 Murray Ross Parkway, tel: 416-736-1733, May to end of December 10am–5pm) is like stepping into the time-warp of mid-19th-century Canada. This charming 'country village' has been recreated to offer a glimpse into the lifestyle of Toronto's early settlers. Country roads and wooden sidewalks snake their way through this quaint village of over 35 homes and workshops. Visitors can wander through the tranquil village, gaining insight into rural Canadian life. There is a 19th-century printing office and a weaver's shop whose wools are dyed by the vegetables from the outlying gardens.

A focal point of the village, Roblin's Mill is powered by a huge wooden water wheel, its millstones grinding wheat into flour exactly as it was done 120 years ago. Black Creek is speckled with artisan shops where trades are still carried out by hand, including blacksmithing, clock-making, tinsmithing, broom-making and barrel-making. If you wander by the Half Way House, you are bound to be lured by the smell of fresh-baked bread and other homemade eats.

Gardens and surrounding greenery are abundant, abloom in spring and ablaze in fall. The village also hosts a variety of special events such as the Spring Fair, corn roasts, apple-baking contests, pumpkin parties, craft demonstrations and sales, theatrical and musical performances, and from mid November to 24 December, children flock to the vast array of special Christmas activities.

Roblin's Mill

★★ **The Canadian National Exhibition** (Exhibition Park, Lakeshore Boulevard between Strachan and Dufferin, tel: 416-393-600) runs for 18 days in August. The exhibition came from the era of grand agricultural and industrial fairs and is indeed one of the world's oldest and largest jamborees of this ilk still operating. Although modern demands have altered the face somewhat, the CNE still manages to retain the excitement and old-world charm of a country fair coming to town.

The 'Ex' has had a long history of firsts, including being the first place for electric streetlights and streetcars to be shown off in Canada. It also offers a jangle of vertigo-inducing rides and all the bells and whistles of a bona fide amusement park, as well as an airshow which buzzes overhead during the fair.

The grounds are open year round for events such as the Royal Agricultural Winter Fair, the Home Show and the Boat Show, housed in the buildings during the months excluding August. A long tradition of summer fairgrounds has secured the status of the buildings in the area; now protected as heritage sites, they are no longer in danger of becoming replaced by more profitable ventures considering their prime, waterfront locale.

The largest house ever built in Canada, ★★★ **Casa Loma** (1 Austin Terrace, tel: 416-923-1171, daily 9.30am–4pm, call ahead to confirm) is a remarkable home, completed in 1914 and inspired by the intricacies of a European medieval castle and the crazy dream of Sir Henry Pellatt. A shrewd businessman, Pellatt was also noted for his penchant for chivalry, the soldier's life and military glory.

Casa Loma

Designed by Toronto's legendary E.J. Lennox (of Old City Hall and King Edward Hotel fame), Casa Loma (Spanish for House on the Hill), as it was dubbed by Lennox's second wife, remains an anomaly in Toronto's urban landscape. The turreted and high-chimneyed structure cuts through the edge of the escarpment, looking down on its surroundings with appropriate grandeur.

The story of Casa Loma reads like a soap opera: the rise and crashing fall of one man's wealth and dreams all tied to a lavishly opulent castle; even the stables were excessively overbuilt with high-reaching turrets and interiors made of rich mahogany and floored in Spanish tile. With over 98 rooms, the 'house' took almost three years to build. The Oak Drawing Room – with its oak panelling and deeply coved ceiling, enriched by elegant carved plaster mouldings – is said to be the most beautiful room of its period in Toronto. A mere 10 years after Casa Loma's construction, Sir Henry was broke and living alone in a dismal industrial suburb. The city eventually took possession in lieu of unpaid taxes, and today visitors are welcome to stroll through the grounds, the castle, the stables and the beautifully kept gardens.

Casa Loma also stages the National Ballet School's *Sugar Plum Fairy* each November.

For those interested in the sublime landscapes of Canadian art's founding painters, a trip to the ★★ **McMichael Gallery** (Islington Avenue, Kleinburg, tel: 905-893-1121, Tuesday to Saturday 10am–4pm, Sunday 10am–5pm) is essential. A short drive northwards from the Pearson International Airport leads to the quaint village of Kleinburg, the home of one of the largest displays of 20th-century Canadian art. The setting is pure Canadiana and couldn't be more appropriate for the collection housed inside. A rustic log and stone building, the gallery is surrounded by 40 hectares (100 acres) of conservation land that overlooks a lush river valley. Emblazoned trees surround the gallery in the fall, snow blankets and dusts the evergreens in winter, and in summer the grounds are fragrant with wild flowers and willowy, tall grasses.

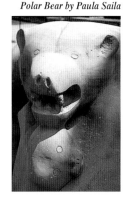
McMichael Gallery: Polar Bear by Paula Saila

56

The McMichael is devoted to showcasing Canadian art and houses works by Tom Thomson and the Group of Seven, along with First Nations, Innuit and contemporary artists. The Group of Seven's work became the touchstone for Canadian landscape painters: the band of painters worked *en plein air* in the 1920s, carting their paintboxes into Canada's wilderness and sketching in the bush to capture the energy and organic nature of the landscape.

The gallery also houses visiting exhibitions of the same ilk: indigenous artwork inextricably linked to Canada's vast landscapes.

Few large cities are without a zoo, and Toronto is no exception. The ★★ **Toronto Zoo** (361A Old Finch Avenue, Scarborough, tel: 416-392-5900, open daily except 25 December, hours vary according to season) is just off Highway 401 at the Meadowvale Road exit, after which there are signs to lead the way. Situated on 4,700 hectares (11,600 acres), the zoo is the largest urban park in North America. It was one of the first to attempt to recreate natural habitats, and the collection of 5,000 animals was also one of the first to be categorised by region of origin and not by type.

The zoo is well-mapped and signed, but due to its expanse, it is impossible to see everything in one visit – much better to select certain areas to cover and focus on them.

Real animals at the zoo

Another option is the Zoomobile, an open-air tram that takes visitors directly to some of the harder-to-reach pavilions. There is also a monorail ride which takes 40 minutes to encircle the perimeter.

★★★ **Ontario Place** (955 Lakeshore Boulevard West, tel: 416-314-9000, mid May to first weekend of September, hours vary according to the date) has been called an oddity among Toronto's modern buildings because it was designed to 'amuse rather than impress'. Spanning three artificial islands with five pod-like structures poised on long legs above the waters of the lake, this multi-faceted complex is an unconventional amusement park, children's playground, marina and trade-tourism pavilion, dreamed up and run by the province of Ontario. Ontario Place defies traditional constructs and has been called everything from 'exuberantly frivolous' to 'distinguished architecturally'.

Ontario Place

With its serene lakeside setting, the area has managed to evade Disneyland commercialism and emerge as an invigorating and relatively inexpensive way to spend a day. If you have kids in tow, Ontario Place is the mecca of play: the Children's Village Playground is an innovative complex jam-packed with everything from the slippery water slides of the amazing Waterplay Park, to the free-of-charge Lego Pod. The showpiece is the Cinesphere theatre, a geodesic dome that shows IMAX movies, and, when lit up at night, casts its bejewelled glitter on to the waters of Lake Ontario.

57

A popular attraction is the ★ **Ontario Science Centre** (770 Don Mills Road, tel: 416-696-3127, open daily except 25 December, 10am–6pm), only 10 minutes from downtown. Due to its diversity and its five sprawling levels, the centre manages to cater for all ages.

Ontario Science Centre

The interactive exhibits range from rock-climbing, to tests that show how well your memory works – all in a spirit that conveys the excitement and intrigue that motivates professional scientists in their work. Visitors can walk through a recreated coral reef, trek though a tropical rainforest, or wander around a limestone cave in the Living Earth exhibit. Live demonstrations include watching a laser beam cut through glass, peeking at the solar system in the planetarium, and observing how a flower can shatter into icy shards.

Special exhibitions surface regularly, and range from explorations of human nature to travelling in the Arctic, often enriched by engaging lectures to well-packed audiences. The new gift store, Mastermind, offers a wide selection of books, software, science kits and other educational toys, as well as kites and precious stones.

Excursion 1

Niagara Falls and Niagara-on-the-Lake

By far the single-most popular day trip for Toronto visitors, ★★★ **Niagara Falls** is justifiably considered one of the seven natural wonders of the world.

The easiest route to the waterfall, which is one of North America's top attractions, is to drive from Toronto following Lake Ontario's southwestern coastline along the Queen Elizabeth Way (QEW), a journey of about 75 minutes. Alternatively, VIA Rail operates trains between Toronto and New York, stopping in St Catharines and Niagara Falls (tel: 416-366-8411).

Despite the kitschy tourist trade – amusement parks, casino, wax museums, daredevil feats, millions of motels complete with a honeymoon suite with a heart-shaped bed – long thriving off the area, the falls remain a spectacular sight unto themselves. It really is impossible for a photograph to replicate the spine-tingling feeling of watching the cascade pound into the river, the permanent misty spray hanging in the air, or hearing the crashing roar of water echoing through the area.

The falls have undoubtedly had a profound influence on the region. From North America's earliest days of exploration a native legend described a mighty waterfall hidden in the middle of the continent, which soon became known as Niagara, a First Nations word thought to mean The Strait (although some have construed it as the more dramatic Thunder of Waters).

The combined flow of the falls is close to 3.5 million litres (800,000 gallons) per second. Along with spurring on the tourist trade, the force of the water has also been harnessed into hydroelectric generating stations on the

Niagara River, which provide power for a significant part of northeastern North America.

For a close look at the thunderous falls, the decks of the now almost legendary **Maid of the Mist** (tel: 905-358-5781) provide an in-your-face view of the turbulent waters. The thrilling journey, which is undertaken from mid-May to mid October, leaves passengers soaked but invigorated from the privileged vantage point.

Another popular option, particularly with the honeymooning crowd, is to view the falls at night. The waterfall is lit by 22 xenon gas spotlights in a wide spectrum of colour, with fireworks adding to the drama every Friday. British man of letters Oscar Wilde, referring to the falls' honeymooning popularity, characteristically felt that they were 'the second biggest disappointment of American married life', to which Marilyn Munroe retorted many years later, 'The falls produce a lot of electricity, but the honeymooners don't use very much of it at night.' Either way, they are definitely the defining feature in an area saturated with attractions.

There is no shortage of things to do besides ogle the falls. Niagara is a place for history buffs, nature enthusiasts and wine-tasters alike. For naturalists, the whole region is unique geographically as it contains more than half of the 139 species of Canada's rare, threatened and

Maid of the Mist

59

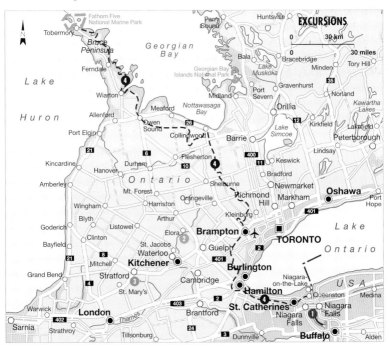

Fruit stand on Niagara Parkway

Musketeers at Fort George

endangered plants and animals. Most of the area is Carolinian forest, which thrives on the mild climate created by the shelter of Lakes Ontario, Erie and Huron, and is named after vegetation that is also found in North and South Carolina.

North of Niagara Falls, the **Niagara Parkway** offers one of the most scenic routes in North America. The botanical gardens of the Niagara School of Horticulture are en route, as are some beautiful farms. In the summer the trees hang heavy with ripening apples, peaches and cherries, often for sale at roadside stands.

The area is also increasingly gaining popularity for its burgeoning wine industry. The wine route winds around picturesque valleys, through countless wineries which all open their doors and vineyards to visitors. Tours and further information can be found through the Wine Council of Ontario (110 Hannover Drive, Suite B205, St Catharines, Ontario, tel: 905-684-8070).

At the end of the Parkway is another treasure of the area: the historically rich ★★★ **Niagara-on-the-Lake**. A beautiful, immaculately preserved and kept 19th-century village resonant with architectural heritage, it has a well-developed theatre tradition, exquisite shops and fine dining. The tree-lined streets, flanked with winsome clapboard and stately brick period houses, create the perfect backdrop for the town's annual ★★ **Shaw Festival** – a renowned theatre festival that began in the 1960s focusing on the plays of George Bernard Shaw and his contemporaries. Niagara-on-the-Lake was actually a sleepy town until the festival began to draw a steady trickle of tourists. It is essential to get tickets in advance (box office, tel: 1-800-511-7429), even though the season now stretches from April to November with an extensive number of performances.

A stroll down Queen Street is a good way to explore the stores that line the sidewalks. The turn-of-the-century shops house everything from homemade jam and fudge, to galleries selling contemporary Canadian crafts. There is also a vast array of eateries and pubs offering excellent food, all in keeping with the 19th-century ambiance.

Before leaving the Niagara area, there is still **Fort George National Historic Park** to explore (Niagara Parkway, tel: 905-468-6614, 1 April to 31 October, daily 10am–5pm; July and August, Saturdays 10am–8pm). History buffs will enjoy this fort, which played a key role in the War of 1812, until the Americans invaded and destroyed it in May 1813, after occupying the town for 11 days. The fort was rebuilt in 1815, abandoned in 1828 and not reconstructed until the 1930s. Visitors are welcome to wander around the officers' quarters, common soldiers' barracks and the guard room with its hard plank beds.

Excursion 2

The Elora Gorge

Elora *See map on page 59*

Situated on the banks of the Grand River, the quaint town of ★★ **Elora** is a tranquil respite from the urban pull – a mere two hours northeast of Toronto. Venerated for its beautiful stone architecture and breathtaking gorge, Elora has a charm and natural beauty that continually lure visitors – not to mention movie and television crews. The most direct route to the town is by taking the 401 Highway west from Toronto, then following Highway 6 north through Guelph which eventually leads to Elora.

The first white settler to arrive at Elora was Rosewell Matthews in 1817. Fifteen years later Captain William Gilkison bought 5,668 hectares (14,000 acres) of land, choosing the location for the great falls that would provide water power to run the mills he hoped to build. From a sea-faring family, he named the village Elora after his brother's new ship, which in turn had been named after the famous Temple Caves of Elora near Bombay, India.

Elora's Dalby House, built in 1835

Gorge trail

Long before the lands of the Grand River were bought and sold by these settlers, as early as the 17th century, First Nations people had been in the area. The Attawanderonk tribe lived so harmoniously off the land that barely a trace was left by them, despite centuries of being here.

Home to the Attawanderonks, the valley of the Grand River also became the ground over which neutral nations fled during the Iriquois terror, beginning in 1684. These tumultuous times forced many women, children, elderly and sick into hiding provided by the caves and ravines of Elora.

It is here that many of the precious wampum beads (which were used as currency) were hidden for safe-keeping, only to be discovered more than 200 years later

Lover's Leap

by First Nations people, who had heard tales of beautiful treasures cached by their forefathers. In 1888, two young boys found the remaining 17th-century wampum beads, which had been washed from the cave by an unusually heavy rain. Some of these are now housed in the Art Gallery of Ontario (*see pages 30–1*).

The rock junction of the Grand and Irvine rivers, known as Lover's Leap, is another reminder of the area's Native associations. Legend tells of an Indian maiden who, after her lover had been killed in battle, threw herself from the rock into the swirling waters below in order to be re-united with him.

Carved by retreating glacial melt waters, Elora's dramatic 21m (69ft)-deep gorge is now a highlight for its spectators year in year out, as well as for avid fly fishermen and thrill-seeking kayakers. Pathways with rail guards hug the cedar-lined banks, along which are strewn caves, rapids and waterfalls, in which Natives believed their spirits lived. Sections of the trails are rough with loose gravel and often wet, so hiking boots or sturdy shoes are advisable.

Elora is also home to one of Canada's few remaining five-storey grist mills, which was saved from abandonment in 1974 and has since been restored into a five-star inn. **The Elora Mill Inn** (77 Mill Street West, tel: 519-846-5356) sits on the most beautiful and dramatic parcel of land in the village. Overlooking the cliff-lined gorge of the Grand River, which is floodlit at night, it offers a spectacular view while enjoying food or drink.

Each of the seasons has distinct appeal for guests as they dine: in winter the water forms gigantic icicles curving and jutting dynamically over the gorge; in spring it is fast flowing; in summer the area is alive with blooming flowers; and fall is a dramatic pastiche of burnt oranges, lemon yellows and fiery reds.

Inside, a wood-beamed ceiling emulates the feel of a rural English pub, with dining rooms bedecked in wood floors, enormous ceiling beams, handmade pine chairs and huge fireplaces. Sometimes there are jazz groups and other bands playing live at the weekend, but it is best to call beforehand to confirm.

A leisurely stroll through the town offers a glimpse of the historic limestone architecture that characterises the beauty of Elora. Speckled with gourmet restaurants, gift shops and boutiques, it is conducive to leisurely browsing while absorbing the antique charm of the buildings.

An especially fruitful time to arrive is mid summer, when the town plays host to an innovative music festival. This is noted for staging performances in unusual venues, such as the local quarry (Elora Music Festival, tel: 519-846-0331, elora@sentex.net).

The Elora Mill Inn

Excursion 3

Stratford *See map on page 59*

Somehow it must have been a prescripted fate that the small Ontario town of ★★★ **Stratford** should end up as the home of the world-famous Shakespearean theatre extravaganza, the **Stratford Festival**. The fact that the town has a picturesque Avon River complete with elegant white swans winding its way through the serene country landscape, or that an aerial photograph revealed that the English garden planted in 1904 to contain every flower mentioned in the plays of Shakespeare, is almost identical to the park in Stratford-upon-Avon, England, seems a little too coincidental.

Talk of the town: William Shakespeare

Stratford lies about 90 minutes southwest of Toronto, and can be reached by taking Highway 401 west to interchange 35, then 90 north on Highway 8 and west again on the combined Highways 7/8. VIA Rail (tel: 416-366-8411) also has trains leaving from Toronto's Union Station at least twice a day during Stratford's peak season. Or there are buses that leave from the Dundas and Bay Streets terminal (tel: 416-393-7911), although they meander into a much lengthier route. Regardless of the mode of transport, the trip is definitely worth the short time it takes to get there.

The town began with rather modest origins: when surveyors came to a marshy creek surrounded by a thick forest in 1812, they called it 'Little Thames' which was later christened Stratford (supposedly meaning 'narrow crossing'). The town kept its rough-hewn backwoods image for the most part until Stratford-born journalist Tom Patterson, after noting that the town wards and schools had names like Hamlet, Falstaff and Romeo, felt that some sort

The Avon River

of drama festival might possibly resurrect his hometown. Capturing the imaginations of the theatre-hungry, Patterson eventually managed to lure renowned British director Tom Guthrie and stage and screen star Alec Guinness, to begin a world-class theatre festival that saw a surprisingly large turn-out to its stuffy little tent performance in 1953. Innovation turned into tradition and the festival instantly catapulted to international success.

The Festival Theatre

The Stratford Festival season runs roughly from May to late October, with performances every day including matinées. Along with the solid Shakespearean contingent performed by the *crème de la crème* of Canadian theatre, a mélange of modern theatrical productions such as *West Side Story*, *Death of a Salesman* and the occasional original piece by a Canadian playwright are on the bill.

The festival is also packed with ancillary events, including backstage tours, free concerts, lectures, University-credited courses, conferences, workshops and readings by celebrated writers and playwrights, to name a few. The Stratford Festival Administration and Information (55 Queen Street, Stratford, Ontario, tel: 519-271-4040 or 1-800-567-1600) is a good place to call when deciding what to see, ticket availability and any other general information relating to the festival.

64

The crowded tent of 1953 has evolved into three main venues: the **Festival Theatre** (55 Queen Street), the **Avon Theatre** (99 Downie Street) and the **Tom Patterson Theatre** (111 Lakeside Drive). The Festival Theatre is located amid rolling parklands by the Avon River and is the largest, complete with an Elizabethan-inspired 'thrust' stage (with the audience surrounding it on three sides). The construction of this permanent theatre marked the culmination of the Stratford Festival dream. Challenged to create a venue that would continue to capture the creative spirit of the festival's landmark tent, the Toronto architect Robert Fairfield put forth a bold 'big-top' design which, in 1958, won the Massey Gold Medal for architecture.

The Avon Theatre

The elegant turn-of-the-century-ish Avon Theatre is centrally located downtown, while the riverside Tom Patterson Theatre is a smaller, more intimate affair with an extended thrust stage.

Although excellent theatre is the main attraction of Stratford, the town itself has blossomed into a bustling spot where entertainment possibilities of all kinds abound.

Libation-seeking visitors will be happy to know that the town has been besieged by quaint, English-style pubs which offer a cool respite in the hot summer months. Sun-flecked outdoor cafés and patios are another relaxing option. The town is also a cornucopia of culinary delights – all in response to the demands of increasing numbers of hungry theatre-going out-of-towners. Everything from pub fare to five-star dining is available, with this eclectic mix ranging from Elizabethan-inspired ambiances, to Mediterranean-influenced menus.

For those inclined to browse the boutiques, the area is strewn with interesting little antique shops, bookstores, shops selling Shakespearean and theatre-related wares, and clothes boutiques – some with the 'cross-century' dressing possibilities of medieval, Napoleonic, Victorian and Edwardian garb.

A festival town full of fine restaurants and boutiques

There are at least five galleries in Stratford. But on Wednesday, Saturday and Sunday from May to the end of September, artists display and sell their creations under the breezy willows that line the Avon River near the Island Bridge known as **Art in the Park of Stratford** (Lakeside Drive and Front Street, tel: 519-225-2962) .

Other highlights of the area include: **Historic Walking Tours** (tel: 519-271-5140), the **St Jacob's Farmers' Market & Flea Market** (where Weber meets King Street, tel: 519-747-1830, Thursday and Saturday 7am–3.30pm year round, plus Tuesday, June to August) where 400 vendors sell fresh meats, cheese, produce, baking and crafts in a large indoor/outdoor country market complete with animals, a picnic area and horse-drawn trolley tours.

Farm produce

Brimming with possibilities, visitors are often obliged to stay overnight in order to pack in all of Stratford's offerings. Accommodation is plentiful, though places often require reservations in the peak season (Tourism Stratford, tel: 1-800-561-SWAN). There are in fact more than 500 hotel/motel rooms, and more bars, restaurants, gift shops, pubs and boutiques than one would imagine for a town with little more than 26,000 residents. There are also dozens of bed and breakfasts, all with picturesque backdrops and often set in beautiful mansions.

Mennonite boys at the Farmers' Market

Long shadows on a long walk

Excursion 4

The Bruce Trail *See map on page 59*

Across the Niagara Escarpment

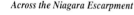

Although Toronto is Canada's largest urban centre, wild spaces remain easily accessible for those looking for a long, satisfying hike. The ★★ **Bruce Trail** is just that: a 770-km (480-mile) trail that traverses the scenic **Niagara Escarpment**. The majestic escarpment carves its way north from Queenston near Niagara Falls towards the water's edge at Tobermory, with its variety of terrain and scenery creating some of the most spectacular walking, hiking and climbing to be found in southern Ontario.

A continuous footpath stretching along the Niagara Escarpment from Niagara to Tobermory was an idea that met with such enthusiasm that it prompted the formation of a special committee, who by 1967 had made the idea a reality. Hikers, climbers, bikers and campers interested in detailed information can refer to the *Guide to the Bruce Trail*, now in its 18th edition. Compiled by the Bruce Trail Association (Hamilton, Ontario, tel. 416-529-6821), it is available at hiking and outdoor outfitters in Toronto.

It is possible to pick up the trail at any number of points, including the **Caledon Hills** section. Only an hour northwest of Toronto following Highway 401 westbound, this area is popular with city hikers looking for a nearby retreat. There are clearly marked footpaths that hug the Credit River and meander across cedar-covered hills, eventually leading to the Bruce Trail. If a big meal is the desired reward after a long hike, there are many country inns dotting the area, including the historic Cataract Inn (1498 Cataract, Caledon, tel: 519-927-3033).

Visitors who don't mind driving a couple of hours northwest of Toronto will be well rewarded with challenging hiking, mountain biking and rock-climbing throughout the summer, and cross-country and downhill skiing in the winter in the **Grey Bruce** area – including the Bruce Trail sections found near Collingwood and the Beaver Valley. The quickest way to reach it is to follow the Highway 400 north, exiting at Highway 26 which meanders its way to Collingwood.

The trail near Collingwood

A playground for the actively inclined, **Kolapore** is located 1.2km (¾ mile) south of the point where the trail crosses Grey County Road 2 (8th Line). The area offers a wide variety of well-marked trails, many of which are loops. Ideal for hiking and mountain biking in the summer months, the trails double as prime cross-country ski tracks in winter.

Kolapore is also home to the **University of Toronto's Outing Club** which keeps a cabin here and shuttles rock-climbers and hikers to the area throughout the whole year. The village of Kolapore once existed as a bustling mill centre which began in the 1860s, with its first sawmill built in 1865. Eventually the village saw several such mills, a number of which operated on water power from the Kolapore Creek.

67

The **Beaver Valley** section of the Bruce Trail can be picked up at Swiss Meadows atop Blue Mountain. The spot offers a vantage point surveying Collingwood, Nottawasaga Bay, Meaford and Thornbury. Trekking west through the rocky gorges and limestone caves of the **Kolapore Uplands** leads to the spectacular view from the cliffs at Old Baldy, eventually landing on the doorstep of the village of **Kimberley**. Sitting in the thick of Beaver Valley, Kimberley is punctuated by the Beaver River which runs southwesterly from Thornbury, through lush agricultural land laden with apple orchards. The river served as a thoroughfare for European settlers who travelled by canoe to Eugenia in the 1850s. The abundance of beavers in the area eventually became the namesake of the valley.

Abandoned barn

Due to the sheer expanse of land encompassed by the Bruce Trail, it is advisable to obtain maps and guides for the various hiking trails. These are made available at visitor and tourist information centres throughout the region and/or can be obtained by calling the Bruce Trail Association (1-800-665-HIKE).

Aside from the physical benefits and the spectacular scenery of hiking along the Bruce Trail, this whole region is also a geologist's paradise. The Niagara Escarpment dates back some 430 million years and showcases some of the best-exposed fossils and rocks of the Paleozoic era. Also of note is the extensive variety of plants and animals en route, some of which are rare or found nowhere else in Ontario.

Architecture

Settled by the British in 1793, Toronto was initially just a muddy-streeted village with precarious wooden dwellings. But it didn't take long before the impressive churches and public structures of European influence began to emerge in what was previously Canadian wild. By 1834 Toronto had gained both status as a fully fledged city and a classical two-storey brick courthouse and a jail, which lent an air of civility and refinement to the former backwater town.

Between 1834 and 1854 Toronto's population almost quadrupled. The city prospered, and soon the bankers and merchants propelled the direction of architecture towards the industrious, rich monuments of the Victoria age. Built in a barrage of opulent styles – Gothic manor houses, Italianate villas, Romanesque abbeys, Queen Anne cottages – many of these structures still stand today. Other evidence of this newly capitalistic era were the flashy warehouses built along Front Street, some of which shipped pigs, earning Toronto its 'Hogtown' sobriquet.

Osgoode Hall

By this time, a law had been passed to erect only brick structures, which was in part to create the feel of a more permanent, aristocratic town, and partly out of concern for fire prevention. As a result, the city benefits from the permanency of these dwellings today. Non-existent, however, is the row housing that defines cities such as London, New York and even Montreal; Torontonians eschewed it for semi-detached homes, forging a distinct residential heritage.

The last decades of the 19th century saw Toronto emerge as a cultural force. The city was also busy annexing neighbouring villages, not only increasing its population but also resulting in the emergence of new architectural elements. The downtown core of the city began to echo this sense of progress and inspiration, and civic monuments began to rise, including the Provincial Parliament Building, the (Old) City Hall, Royal Ontario Museum, Art Gallery of Toronto (Ontario) and Union Station.

Royal Ontario Museum entrance

Previously, Toronto's urban planners had followed the European aversion to skyscrapers. But debates swirled in the city council on the issue of whether to allow a more American approach or stick to European sensibilities. New World won out, and Toronto elected not to limit height. Immediately, the city set out to erect the tallest building in the British Empire, which resulted in a rash of bank tower buildings. Many of these now pose a *double entendre*: their beauty and classical style is a welcome change from the faceless, modern skyscrapers of glass and metal. However, they sit among these structures in a world for which they were not designed. Preservation is easy enough, but their

function is somehow lost in the changes dictated by the modern world.

Urban development in the United States was dictated after World War I by the automobile and the expressway, and the suburbs which were formed as a result. Toronto followed the American model, building instant suburbs which inevitably changed the inner-city neighbourhoods. When waves of immigrants filtered through, they slipped into the low-scale Victorian residential streets that had been recently vacated, breathing much-needed new life into these areas.

The downtown core of the city has always been kept intact, and is very much the hub of Toronto. It did fall victim to the phase of levelling old buildings, only to have them replaced by skyward-bound pillars of modernity. The city's financial district became scattered with mega-towers, including the Toronto Dominion Centre and the Royal Bank Plaza, and culminating in the world's tallest freestanding structure: the CN Tower.

Although the spire of St James' Cathedral, which once towered over its surroundings, has long been dwarfed by the CN Tower, the city has been enriched by its ability to accommodate both. Since the emergence of post-modernism, the trend has shifted back to the lavish forms of the past. The result is that, though the modern behemoths have long been criticised for their isolation of people from the space that surrounds them, when they share the street with Victorian, Gothic and Edwardian structures they somehow become more human.

Toronto is a not simply a jangle of typical urban architecture. Instead, the scattered nature of the city's architectural history results in a blend of old and new which together create the depth and character of a diversely original cityscape.

Victoriana in Chinatown

The modern skyline

Literature

Toronto seems to breed good literature – that is, if place has something to do with it. A city, in literary terms, is usually an ambiguous landscape into which characters are placed, but Toronto's writers have reclaimed this myth of urban anonymity. Take Margaret Atwood, one of the first female writers to ascribe symbolic value to the city, while maintaining some degree of geographical accuracy. Michael Ondaatje has also written lyrical, impassioned prose describing the building of the Bloor Street Viaduct and the R.C. Harris Water Filtration Plant in his novel *In the Skin of a Lion*.

But this wasn't always the case. Toronto once had a tough time with literature because its writers struggled against either falling into mimicry of imported British literature or the accusation of writing American literature with 'something' missing – not to mention combating the world's image of Canadians residing in teepees blanketed in northern snow. In reality, most Canadians live in cities, yet the telling of urban experience was previously terrain reserved for European and American authors only.

Despite these difficulties, writers emerged in Toronto, many of whom were published by the now-defunct House of Ryerson Press. But it wasn't until the 1960s that writers catapulted the city to international literary acclaim. In an attempt to shed its puritanical Victorian roots, Toronto began to struggle from the grip of cultural colonialism and write its own script. Small literary presses surfaced, publishing indigenous poetry and novels, and leapfrogging into uncharted ground.

It was the writers of this era who created a rich cultural legacy for Toronto and the rest of Canada – they *were* the literary canon. The list of them reads like a *Who's Who* of the literary world: Margaret Atwood, Michael Ondaatje, Robertson Davies, Morley Callahan, Gwendolyn MacEwan and Dennis Lee, and the newer crop of Barbara Gowdy, Anne Michaels, Anne-Marie MacDonald and many more. In fact, most of Canada's best-known writers presently live within a few dozen blocks of one another in the City of Toronto.

One of the most polyglot, multicultural and multiracial cities anywhere, Toronto's position as literary giant is understandable in its modern context. As described by Anne Michaels in her award-winning novel *Fugitive Pieces*, 'It's a city where almost everyone has come from elsewhere... bringing with them their different ways of dying and marrying, their kitchens and songs.' And so the city has come alive in all its facets, supported by publishing houses, literary festivals, cultural events *(see pages 74–5)* and, ultimately, great authors.

A vital part of the culture

Performing Arts

Theatre

Toronto is the theatre capital of Canada. It ranks the third most significant centre of English-speaking theatre production in the world (behind only London and New York), and is laced with theatres, of both the blockbuster and non-profit-making alternative kind. Full-scale productions play to sold-out theatres, while the alternative scene is cultivating a following of its own.

From the 1960s, the mega-productions of Garth Drabinsky and Ed Mirvish almost single-handedly created and maintained Toronto's theatre district. Drabinsky was responsible for several acclaimed shows, including *Kiss of the Spider Woman* and a revival of *Show Boat*, both of which garnered Tony Awards on Broadway. Mirvish has backed several successful musicals housed in the legendary Royal Alexandra Theatre, which he meticulously restored to its original splendour (*see page 24*).

The Pantages Theatre

When Canada Council promoted arts and culture from the 1960s through to the 1980s, Toronto allowed the indigenous talent to have a voice to speak the Canadian experience. Theatre began to mirror the multicultural fabric of Canadian society, echoing the lifestyles and concerns of everyone from first-generation immigrants to truck drivers to drag queens. While the 1960s and 1970s exploded with alternative theatre, the early 1980s were dominated by smaller, even more avant-garde companies. The decade also marked the expansion of the commercial scene with such mega-musicals as *Cats, Les Misérables, Phantom of the Opera* and *Tommy*; shows like *Sunset Boulevard* followed in the 1990s.

Theatres that showcase commercial plays and musicals include the following: **Elgin and Winter Garden Theatres**, 189 Yonge Street, tel: 416-314-2871; **Pantages Theatre**, 263 Yonge Street, tel: 416-872-2222; **Princess of Wales Theatre**, 300 King Street West, tel: 416-872-1212; and **The Royal Alexandra Theatre**, 260 King Street West, tel: 416-872-1212.

Theatre Passe Muraille and Buddy in Bad Times

For smaller, more avant-garde productions, consider the following: **Tarragon Theatre**, 30 Bridgman Avenue, tel: 416-531-1827; **The Factory Theatre**, 125 Bathurst Street, tel: 416-504-9971; or **Theatre Passe Muraille**, 16 Ryerson Avenue, tel: 416-504-7529. These theatres are Toronto's equivalent of off-Broadway – well-established venues where a mind-boggling array of topics, styles and approaches are innovatively performed. Here you can observe a freedom of expression that is the cornerstone of alternative theatre. Also of note is **Buddies in Bad Times Theatre** (12 Alexander Street, tel: 416-975-8555), home of the Rhubarb Theatre Festival, which produces more gay and lesbian plays than any other venue on the continent.

Music and dance

Roy Thompson Hall

Classical music has long graced the concert halls and churches of the city. Holding the spotlight is the venerable Toronto Symphony Orchestra, which has provided the city with textured classical programming for over 75 years. Toronto's great musical virtuoso, the pianist Glenn Gould (1932–82), made his début with this orchestra at the tender age of 14. Showcasing a broad range of composers over a lengthy season, the TSO plays at the **Roy Thompson Hall** (60 Simcoe Street, box office tel: 416-872-4255).

73

Toronto's world-famous Baroque orchestra, **Tafelmusik** (tel: 416-964-6337), is a period-instrument ensemble which beautifully interprets Bach, Vivaldi *et al*, with performances between fall and spring in places such as Trinity-St Paul's United Church, Bloor Street West. In the chamber music department, **Music Toronto** provides ongoing concerts by visiting ensembles at the **St Lawrence Centre for the Arts** (21 Front Street, tel: 416-368-3110).

The Canadian Opera Company, whose repertoire is a rich and varied pastiche of composers, is a resident of the **Hummingbird Centre for the Performing Arts**, also home to the National Ballet of Canada (1 Front Street East, tel. 416-393-7469). The smaller **Opera Atelier** has heralded international acclaim for its authentic period performances of operatic and dance pieces from composers such as Purcell and Rameau.

Home of the National Ballet

Another option for live performances is the **Ford Centre for the Performing Arts** (5040 Yonge Street, tel: 416-872-2233), which features everything from opera to jazz to Latin rhythms.

Harbourfront is a flurry of dance activity, with cutting-edge performances at the **Premiere Dance Theatre** (207 Queen's Quay West, tel: 416-973-4000) by a full range of companies, including the Toronto Dance Theatre and Les Ballets Jazz.

Festivals

The mark of a vibrant city is a wealth of things to do, and nowhere is Toronto's vibrancy more evident than on its calendar, which is jam-packed with events and festivals.

Starting in November is the **Royal Agricultural Winter Fair**, the largest indoor agricultural and equestrian event in the world. For Christmas, Toronto's City Hall hosts the **Cavalcade of Lights**, including a carol concert and New Year celebration in Nathan Phillips Square.

In a completely different vein is the **Psychics, Mystics and Seers' Fair**, held in early-February at Exhibition Place. Also in February is the **Toronto Festival of Storytelling** at the Harbourfront Centre, infused with workshops, concerts and free afternoon storytelling, and attracting over 70 storytellers from Canada and elsewhere.

March is enlivened when all of the city's Irish crowd come out for the **St Patrick's Day Parade** downtown.

Just when the city begins to bloom, the **Victoria Day Musical Fireworks** are held at Ontario Place on the fourth Monday in May. Toronto celebrates the former Queen's birthday in a spectacular display of fireworks set to music, evidence of its long-standing ties with England.

June marks the beginning of an event-laden summer. Kicking off the month is the **Milk International Children's Festival**, which is North America's largest performing arts festival catering for the entire family. Spanning a week, it offers theatre, dance, music, visual arts, storytelling, physical comedy and puppetry. A month-long festival also in June, **Northern Encounters** showcases traditional music, arts and culture of Canada and other members of the Arctic Council.

Bloom in the Beaches, a literary festival, is in full swing by mid June, along with the **Du Maurier Downtown Jazz**, a festival featuring over 1,500 international and Canadian musicians playing at a variety of venues throughout the city. Of great acclaim is June's **Toronto International Caravan**, which offers great food and drink and 50 pavilions displaying terrific ethnic music and dance throughout the city. June also draws race-track aficionados for the **Queen's Plate**, an internationally renowned horse race at Toronto's Woodbine Racetrack.

Towards the end of June, more than 100,000 spectators converge on Centre Island for the **Toronto International Dragon Boat Race Festival**. Held over two days, the festival combines culture and sports with more than 30 multicultural, ethnic group performances. Around 170 teams from all over the world compete in the races, making this the largest dragon boat event in the world.

July's **Toronto Outdoor Art Exhibition** is a free outdoor exhibition held in Nathan Phillips Square, which

Downtown jazz

showcases the original paintings, ceramics, jewellery, sculpture and mixed-media creations of a diverse grouping of Canadian and international artists. In late-July, the sultry Latin rhythms, energised sounds of calypso and laconic drawls of jazz riffs swirl in the streets of the Beaches at the **Beaches International Jazz Festival**.

Theatre is thriving in the summer months too. The latest addition is the **Fringe of Toronto Festival**, which supports 10 days of theatre at various venues in and around the Annex area.

Bringing in the month of August is **Caribana**, a citywide version of a carnival which infuses the streets with Caribbean and Latin American flare and is one of Toronto's most colourful events. Other August events include the **Circle Ball Fair** which offers 10 days of busking competitions, and the **Fringe Festival of Independent Dance Artists** held at the Buddies in Bad Times Theatre.

Caribana colour and dragon boat fever

The second half of August is dominated by the **Canadian National Exhibition** (CNE), when the fairgrounds become home to one of the world's largest and longest annual exhibitions. An 18-day extravaganza, the 'Ex' features rides, free shows, grandstand performances, and the three-day Canadian International Air Show.

With fall comes an onslaught of the literati, including the **Word On the Street Festival**, an outdoor book fair that features readings, book bargains and activities for children. The **International Festival of Authors** is another popular highlight of the cultural calendar, with both Canadian and international writers coming together to create the world's largest literary festival.

Fall is also the season for the **Toronto International Film Festival** (Festival of Festivals). The city turns into tinsel town itself for 10 days when stars descend to attend a slew of gala parties, openings and screenings.

Food and Drink

Multiculturalism combined with Bay Street dollars has created a city with a richly diverse palate – the exotic flavours of international foods blend with modern sensibilities and innovation, creating an ethnically infused assortment of eateries to choose from. With well over 4,000 restaurants, Toronto has joined the ranks as one of the major culinary capitals of North America. Along with the long-standing Italian, Greek and Chinese population, the new wave of immigrants from Sri Lanka, Indonesia, Ethiopia, Spain, South America and the Middle East has introduced novel intricacies to the city's menus.

Restaurant selection

$$$ expensive ($30 or more per person); $$ moderate ($20–30 per person); $ inexpensive (under $20 per person). Prices do not include wine, tax or gratuities.

Toronto's notables

Boba, 90 Avenue Road, tel: 416-961-2622. A converted house full of small rooms with a globally diverse menu that has caught the attention of many food critics. $$$

Canoe, 66 Wellington Street West, Toronto Dominion Tower, tel: 416-364-0054. Its perch on the 54th floor allows diners a spectacular view of the lake and Toronto Islands. Exquisite local ingredients are cooked with Japanese meticulousness. $$$

Scaramouche, 1 Benvenuto Place, tel: 416-961-8011. This is a popular spot with the culinary élite, with a menu brimming with an innovative cornucopia of flavour cooked to perfection. $$$

360 (in the CN Tower), 301 Front Street West, tel: 416-362-5411. At night the city is like a jewel box from this vertigo-inducing vantage point. $$.

A restaurant with views

Asian

Toronto has two Chinatowns in the centre, the older of which is on Spadina Avenue between College and Dundas Streets and spans both directions along Dundas Street West. The stores and markets in this area spill out into the street with their exotic produce and odorous fresh fish, setting the scene for authentic and delectable Asian cuisine. A recent influx of Vietnamese immigrants has enlivened the scene with their resonant food culture.

Preparing Peking duck

Bangkok Garden, 18 Elm Street, tel: 416-977-6748. The lavish Thai decor, coupled with an extensive menu that includes exotic soups, seafood and stir-fried dishes, makes this a popular stop, especially among theatre-goers after performances at the nearby Elgin and Winter Garden. $$$

Nami, 55 Adelaide Street East, tel: 416-362-7373. A

For traditional Thai

delectable sushi bar, complete with booths, and a top-notch *robata* (raw fish) counter. $$$

Indochine, 4 Collier Street, tel: 416-922-5840. This restaurant showcases the full spectrum of Vietnamese cuisine, including fusions with some outside countries' influences, such as France, Thailand and China. $$

Lee Garden, 331 Spadina Avenue, tel: 416-593-9524. An authentic Chinese dining room with some of the best food in the quarter, including steamed bass with ginger and scallions (spring onions). $$

Young Thailand Restaurant, 165 John Street, tel: 416-593-9291. Traditional dishes from Thailand are found here, including spicy chicken with coconut-milk soup and bamboo shoots, and garlic shrimp and mango salad. $$

Champion House, 480 Dundas Street West, tel: 416-977-8282. Famous for its Peking duck, this restaurant also features a vast array of vegetarian dishes. $

Sushi Bistro, 204 Queen Street West, tel: 416-971-5315. A relatively inexpensive selection of dishes makes this the appropriate venue for sushi neophytes. $

French

In the 1980s, the city was peppered with the pretentious dining rooms of French restaurants. But these have since been replaced with more vibrant and innovative cuisine.

Pastis, 1158 Yonge Street, tel: 416-928-2212. Pastis oozes French atmosphere and culinary magic. Among the delectable choices are: terrine of duck foie gras with a dried fig compote, shelled Nova Scotia lobster accompanied by ricotta gnocchi, and hot caramelised apple tart or roasted pear with hazelnut, chocolate and caramel sauce. $$$

The stylish Arlequin

Arlequin, 134 Avenue Road, tel: 416-928-9251. Patronised by Toronto's literati, this stylish bistro offers mouthwatering daily specials and decadent desserts. $$

Greek

With its first restaurant opening in 1900, Toronto's Greektown has a rich culinary tradition centred around Danforth Avenue. The heavy nature of authentic Greek food – meaty kebabs, greasy *souvlaki* and dizzyingly sugary desserts – has been given a modern, healthier revamp. Danforth (between Broadview and Pape Avenues) is brimming with a wide selection of Greek eateries.

Pan on the Danforth, 516 Danforth Avenue, tel: 416-466-8158. A long list of Greek standbys blended with innovative flavours makes this colourful restaurant special. $$.

The pioneering Ouzeri

Ouzeri, 500A Danforth Avenue, tel: 416-778-0500. A stylish restaurant that was the pioneer of *haute-moderne* Greek cuisine, Ouzeria offers items such as filo pies delicately spiced with anise, cinnamon and mint – along with typically garlicky Greek fare. $

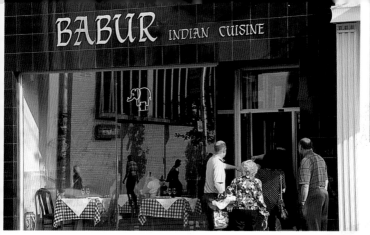

Indian

For a good all-round menu

Toronto's East Indian community has its commercial district on Gerrard Street East between Hiawatha Road and Coxwell Avenue. Here the air is filled with incense and sweet spices from the many restaurants and grocery stores that share the street with outlets selling silks and saris. There are plenty of moderately priced Indian restaurants in the area, although you will find many other excellent Indian eateries sprinkled throughout the city.

Babur, 273 Queen Street West, tel: 416-599-7720. The good all-round menu features northern Indian cooking like tandoori chicken with mango, creamy lamb korma and plenty of vegetarian choices. $

Gujurat Durbar, 1386 Gerrard Street East, tel: 416-406-1085. A fully vegetarian menu with a northwest Indian bent in the heart of the Indian community. $

Italian

A short strip that stretches along College Street from Euclid Avenue to Grace Street, Little Italy is a lively neighbourhood with all the Italian essentials: wines, espresso, herbs and vegetables. There is a vibrant selection of moderately priced restaurants, plus long-established eateries.

Centro Grill and Wine Bar, 2472 Yonge Street, tel: 416-483-2211. This lavishly glamorous restaurant opts for Italian cuisine infused with a lot of California and a splash of Canada (note: caribou chops with cloudberries) – a place to see and be seen. $$$

A cosy setting

Grappa, 797 College Street, tel: 416-535-3337. The cozy setting complements the solid menu, which includes fabulous fresh breads and dishes such as grilled quail and wild boar sausage on black trumpet-mushroom risotto. $$

Trattoria Giancarlo, 41 Clinton Street, tel: 416-533-9619. A favoured haunt located in central Little Italy, complete with romantic patio. $$

A choice of gigs

Some music venues

Nightlife

At night Toronto offers a glut of possibilities. The city is the third-largest centre of English-speaking theatre in the world with both blockbuster and fringe performances playing night after night (*see page 72*). Along with classical music at the large performance halls, there are endless live music options – everything from jazz to alternative music abounds (*see page 73*).

For all forms of pop music, Toronto's independent music scene is, according to Tyler Stewart of the group Barenaked Ladies, 'bustling with amazing groups. Almost any night of the week, [you] can go to The Rivoli or the Horseshoe Tavern and hear stuff that sounds better than anything you're listening to right now on the radio.'

For those who are solely looking for a drink or two, the options range from English-style pubs to glammed-up lounges and everything in between. Because of the infinite options, it is a good idea to check the free weekly entertainment newspapers that appear around the city, such as *Now* and *Eye* magazines.

Bars, pubs and lounges

Bamboo, 312 Queen Street West, tel: 416-593-5771. A rooftop patio offering a tasty selection of Thai/Caribbean food and live music.

Bar Italia, 582 College Street, tel: 416-535-3621. A mainstay in Little Italy with an inviting atmosphere, billiards and jazz upstairs.

Brunswick House, 481 Bloor Street West, tel: 416-924-2242. A long-established raucous, mug-clinking pub.

C'est What?, 67 Front Street East, tel: 416-867-9499. A dark, intimate brew pub with live pop, rock, folk, blues, funk and jazz.

El Macombo, 464 Spadina Avenue, tel: 416-922-1570. The Rolling Stones played here in the 1970s, and it is still an intimate venue to see live music.

El Convento Rico, 750 College Street, tel: 416-588-7800. Lively Latino salsa at this gay and lesbian bar where anyone is welcome.

Guvernment, 132 Queen's Quay East, tel: 416-869-1462. Lounges, cafés and a huge dance floor with live music can all be found at this waterfront warehouse.

Horseshoe Tavern, 368 Queen Street West, tel: 416-598-4753. A legendary beer-swilling venue to see live bands.

Industry, 901 King Street West, tel: 416-260-2660. A 7ft (2m) water fountain, plush lounge area and cutting-edge music attract all-night dance devotees from every walk of life.

Lava, 507 College Street, tel: 416-966-5282. There's lavish decor in this kitsch lounge, with wafting, mellow music that swings from Latin to lounge.

Madison, 14 Madison Avenue, tel: 416-927-1722. A bustling meeting-place popular with both students and the after-work crowd.

Ted's Collision and Body Repair, 573 College Street, tel: 416-533-2430. A bistro and pub that features live bands of every kind.

The Rivoli, 332 Queen Street West, tel: 416-596-1908. Check listings to see who's playing – a worthy venue to see live bands.

A welcoming spot

81

Comedy

Second City, 110 Lombard Street, tel: 416-863-1162. An internationally renowned sketch-comedy company that launched the likes of John Candy and Mike Myers.

Yuk Yuk's, 2335 Yonge Street, tel: 416-967-6425. Canada's largest stand-up comedy venue has seen numerous top-name performers such as Jim Carrey, David Letterman, Jerry Seinfeld and Robin Williams.

Jazz

Jazz and blues have long been entwined with the city's music scene, along with being showcased in the Du Maurier Downtown Jazz and Beaches International Jazz Festivals (*see pages 74–5*). Here are the main venues:

Montreal Bistro and Jazz Club, 65 Sherbourne Street West, tel: 416-363-0179. Expect to unwind to jazz standards played by talented local and visiting musicians.

Rex Hotel, 194 Queen Street West, tel: 416-598-2475. A place to see great jazz, whether it is on a jam-packed Saturday night or a lazy Sunday afternoon.

Top o' the Senator, 253 Victoria Street, tel. 416-364-7517. A congenial atmosphere that showcases adept jazz talent passing through the city.

The Rex

Uptown girls

Shopping

Toronto offers the full spectrum of shopping opportunities, from chic boutiques to mega-malls and everything in between. Ultimately where to go depends on what you're looking for, and what kind of experience you want. Equally strewn throughout the city are gargantuan shopping centres retailing everything imaginable, outdoor markets laden with fresh produce, and old homes within residential neighbourhoods that have been converted into elegant speciality shops and boutiques. There are also funky vintage clothing shops, antique and flea markets, and strings of delis and bakeries sharing streets with second-hand bookshops and one-of-a-kind craft boutiques.

The Eaton Centre

The Eaton Centre

Top billing goes to this gigantic shopping mecca for its sheer size and diversity, not to mention its central location. With over 300 stores, The Eaton Centre (corner of Yonge and Dundas Streets, tel: 416-598-8700, Monday to Friday 10am– 9pm, Saturday 9.30am–6pm, Sunday 12–5pm) has been ranked as the largest downtown shopping mall in North America, and its size will definitely not disappoint energetic shoppers.

With four sprawling levels and a food court tucked below, all under one spectacular roof, the shopping centre has a vast array of mid-priced to high-end stores. Canada's two largest department stores, the Bay and Eaton's, are bookends to the complex. Here shoppers will also find the old standby clothing chains including Gap, Banana Republic, Canada's own Roots and Club Monaco, amid dozens of others. Shoe stores, gift shops, jewellery boutiques, record shops and children's clothing and toy stores are also in abundance.

Bloor Street

Between Yonge Street and Avenue Road, Bloor Street is the locus of Toronto's high-end shopping district. Flanking either side of the street, the boutiques on this strip read like Ivana Trump's roladex: Gucci, Chanel, Versace, Prada and Armani – to name a few. Canada's own Holt Renfrew is also in this area, catering to the *haute-couture* crowd as well as showcasing indigenous clothing designers. This is no regular department store – an impeccably dressed gentleman graciously opens the door and greets shoppers, and, due to Toronto's increasing popularity as a movie locale, celebrity spotting is now commonplace here.

Holt Renfrew for haute-couture

Bloor Street is dotted with boutiques dedicated to health and beauty products, such as Aveda and MAC. Also found in the area are such jewellery giants as Tiffany's, and the fine china and crystal of Ashley's.

For those who are operating on more of a budget, Bloor Street is also home to a handful of moderately priced international clothing chains, including Eddie Bauer, Benetton, Gap, Club Monaco and Roots.

Alternatively, there is always the option of browsing through HMV for CDs, or the three-storey Chapters bookstore near Avenue Road and Bloor.

83

The Annex

In the square formed by Avenue Road to Bathurst Street and Bloor Street West to Dupont Street lies the area known as The Annex. A hippie hangout in the 1960s, it retains much of its creative flair and still plays home to students, professors, writers and members of the art community. The main retail stores are on Bloor, while Georgian and Tudor homes painted in Mediterranean colours speckle the adjacent side streets, adding to the artistic flavour of the neighbourhood. On Markham Street just west of Bathurst is a strip of restored homes housing antique shops, bookstores and a Saturday organic-foods market.

The artsy Annex

Yorkville

Yet another luxury shopping area, Yorkville lies two blocks north of Bloor on Yonge. This upscale neighbourhood lays claim to a barrage of high-end boutiques, rooftop patioed restaurants and well-established independent galleries. Strolling westward along Yorkville Avenue offers a glimpse at the healthy variety of eateries that sit cheek by jowl with fascinating shops. Hazelton Avenue meanders northward through the art contingent here. Many of the galleries in this neighbourhood were the first to nurture new Canadian artists, including Nancy Poole's Studio, Mira Goddard and Sable-Castelli.

Further along the street is the exclusive mall, **Hazelton Lanes** (55 Hazelton Avenue, tel: 416-968-8600), which

Yorkville

houses everything from a two-storey Ralph Lauren boutique to shops offering all manner of speciality gifts, jewellery and *au courant* furnishings.

Yonge Street

The longest street in the world at 1.896km (1.178 miles), Yonge Street has many faces. The most pleasant section for a leisurely stroll lies between Eglinton and Lawrence Avenues. The usual international clothing chains are found here but there is also Sporting Life, a gigantic store carrying sports equipment, clothing and accessories of every kind. The area also has a Future Shop, which offers the gamut of electronics, and the Toronto Children's Bookstore, which shelves the largest collection of children's books in the city.

Sporting Life

Queen Street West

Peach Beserk

For those who shy away from malls and don't like the pretence of upscale labels, there is the lively **Queen Street West** shopping scene *(see Tour 4, page 32)*. Although Gap, Club Monaco, La Cache and The Body Shop make an appearance on the strip, further west leads to funkier, more individual boutiques catering for those with eclectic tastes. Before hitting Spadina Avenue there is Fluevog Shoes, bursting with shoes and boots of a sometimes zany nature.

Continuing west on Queen leads to the bohemian expanse of distinctive shops and boutiques, coffee houses, delis and record stores. The textile shops here sell some of the best vintage clothing in town; many carry well-kept items alongside revamped clothes. Interspersed among these shops are designers who design, sew and sell their creations all under the same small roof, such as at Peach Berserk and Preloved.

Also home to the independent music scene, the area is an appropriate place to hunt down any CDs and vinyl that are hard to find in mainstream record stores. Antiquarian books are also in abundance here and nosing around in the selection of second-hand bookstores can undoubtedly eat up a lot of book lovers' time.

Other vintage items include furniture and collectables of all eras and places: Jalan has higher-end Southeast Asian items, whereas Red Indian and Quasi Modo offer a broad range of vintage furnishings.

Mendocino

College Street

Another trendsetting shopping strip has popped up along College Street between Palmerston and Grace. This area is laden with boutiques housing several of Canada's up-and-coming clothing designers, as well as a number of other independent stores – from eco-friendly shops, to second-hand record stores.

Sports and Recreation

Toronto has been called a sports enthusiast's dream – both for the participant and the spectator. The city is home to four major-league professional teams.

Spectator sports

Baseball has a long tradition here, which began with baseball Hall-of-Famer Babe Ruth hitting his first professional home run in a park on Toronto Island. Since 1977, the **Toronto Blue Jays Baseball Team** (tel: 416-341-1111) have dominated summer sports in the city, with fans flocking to the climate-controlled SkyDome, the only retractable-roofed stadium in North America. The Blue Jays are still remembered for their feat in 1992 and 1993 of becoming the first team not based in the United States to win the World Series in back-to-back seasons.

The SkyDome from above

Another resident of the SkyDome is the Canadian Football League's (CFL) **Toronto Argonauts** (tel: 416-341-5151). Although surrounded by less fanfare than the football league of its neighbours to the south, the CFL is actually two years older than the National Football League, with the Grey Cup a solid fixture for Canadian fans during late November.

Hockey is one of the most venerated Canadian winter sports, and the **Toronto Maple Leafs** have a big local following, selling out the majority of their games even when they sit near the bottom of the National Hockey League (NHL). The Leafs recently left the hallowed Maple Leaf Gardens, one of the oldest rinks of the league, and are now based at the new Air Canada Centre (40 Bay Street at Lakeshore Boulevard, tel: 416-815-5600).

The Maple Leafs win again

The most recent addition to the city's professional sporting ranks is the **Toronto Raptors** (tel: 416-214-2255). Since they joined the National Basketball Association, they've had a young following who are attracted to the flashy atmosphere synonymous with the NBA.

Recreation

There are any number of recreation options. In summer, the Beaches district usually has a game of beach volleyball in motion, as well as a barrage of inline skating, jet skis, sailboards and bicycles taking over the area. There are also plenty of golf courses, tennis courts, public pools and even indoor rock-climbing gyms scattered throughout the city. For those visiting Toronto in the winter months, a whole new range of recreational options have surfaced recently and winter sports abound, from skating at various public rinks or the popular Nathan Phillips Square, to skiing at any number of resorts that dot the areas north of the city, to fishing and hiking.

Getting There

By air

Lester B. Pearson International Airport is situated on the northwest corner of Toronto, 32km (18 miles) from the city centre. The airport houses three terminals. For Terminals 1 and 2, tel: 905-676-3506, and for Terminal 3, tel: 905-612-5100. The phone lines provide information on departure and arrival times, duty-free shops and other airline services.

Various bus and coach lines offer shuttles to downtown Toronto, including Pacific Western (tel: 905-564-6333). The first bus departs from the centre to the airport at 4.40am, the last at 11.30pm; the first departure from the airport to downtown is at 6.30am, the last at 12.55am. Alternatively, limousine services are also readily available at the airport.

Toronto is also served by the **Toronto City Centre Airport**, located at the western tip of one of the Toronto Islands and a convenient option for those staying downtown and flying on to other Canadian destinations. There is a free shuttle service from the Royal York Hotel and a free ferry to the terminal. For flight information, tel: 416-696-5551; and to make reservations, tel: 416-925-2311.

Toronto by air

87

By rail

VIA Rail and **Amtrak** both offer passenger rail services from Union Station, connecting Toronto to the rest of Canada and the United States. The train conveniently rides to the heart of the city. For further information, tel: 1-800-561-3952. VIA Rail provides all services in Canada, with connections to the Amtrak system through Niagara Falls.

Inside Union Station

By bus

The main bus terminal is located on the corner of Bay and Dundas Streets, at 610 Bay Street, in the heart of the city's financial district. Greyhound Lines of Canada operate from here (tel: 416-594-0343) and offer scheduled services across the country. These also link to the Greyhound system in the United States, as well as to other bus companies' networks.

By car

Toronto is linked to the United States by two of the city's major highways. If travelling from New York State, the Queen Elizabeth Way (QEW) is the major artery to Toronto. Those driving from Michigan can enter the city via Highway 401, which hugs the northern section of the city. It can be picked up upon crossing the US/Canada border, and extends to the American border in the west, and Quebec in the east.

Getting Around

Orientation

Toronto is laid out in a grid pattern consisting of major north-south and east-west arteries. The Highway 401, the Don Valley Parkway, the Gardiner Expressway and the Highway 427 create a box around the city.

Subway

Transit options

The TTC (Toronto Transit Commission) is an efficient public transport system consisting of subway, bus, train and streetcar routes snaking their way around the city. Services are clean, safe and inexpensive, and it is possible to combine a subway ride with a bus or streetcar upon purchasing a transfer ticket. Day passes and single-ride tickets or tokens are sold at subway stations and some convenience stores. A family/day pass for unlimited travel is $6.50, an adult day pass $2 (cash only, in exact change); pick up transfers when boarding the vehicle. There are three subway lines: Yonge running north-south, Bloor running east-west, and LRT in the east. Many of the streetcar and bus routes operate 24 hours a day. For information on all routes, schedules and fares, tel: 416-393-4636.

Taxis are always nearby

Taxis

It is fairly easy to hail a cab in the city, particularly in the downtown area. Taxi stands can be found outside major hotels, Union Station and various points throughout the financial district. Meters start running at $2.50.

GO Transit

GO Transit operates a bus/train service to suburban areas and destinations just outside. Day passes and tickets can be bought at stations across the city, with fares charged according to the distance travelled. Tel: 416-869-3200.

Ferry captain

Ferries

To visit the Toronto Islands, catch the ferry from the docks at the foot of Bay Street on Queen's Quay. From Union Station, walk south on Bay Street to The Westin Harbour Castle hotel – the path on the west side of the building leads to the docks. For fares and schedules, tel: 416-392-8193.

Driving

Toronto is relatively straightforward to drive in, but it is advisable to have a map that indicates one-way streets. Parking is a problem as it is very limited downtown and pricey. There are many car rental companies, most of which have offices at the airport and downtown. UK and US drivers must be over 21 to hire a car but need only their national licence. For drink driving, *see page 92.*

Facts for the Visitor

Planning the next move

Travel documents

Visitors from countries other than the United States must have a valid passport to enter Canada. If a stay of over three months is planned, a visa may be required. Consult the Canadian embassy or consulate serving your home country for further details. American citizens and legal residents don't require passports or visas, although they might be asked for proof of citizenship. Naturalised American citizens should carry a naturalisation certificate or other evidence of citizenship. Permanent US residents who are not citizens are advised to bring their Alien Registration Receipt Card.

89

Customs

Visitors from the United States or overseas who are 19 or older are allowed to import duty-free 200 cigarettes, 50 cigars, 400g of manufactured tobacco and 400 tobacco sticks. Also permitted are 1.1 litres (40oz) of liquor or wine, or 8.2 litres (24 x 12oz cans or bottles) of beer, and gifts not exceeding $60 (provided they do not consist of alcohol, tobacco or advertising material). Duty and tax must be paid on the balance if the gifts are worth over $60.

Restrictions also apply to importing certain specialty goods, including meats, dairy products and agricultural products and/or materials. People bringing a pet into the country must present a rabies certificate.

Tourist Information

Tourism Toronto (Queen's Quay Terminal at Harbourfront, Suite 590, 207 Queen's Quay West, Toronto, ON, M5J 1A7, tel: 416-203-2500; 1-800-363-1990, toll-free in North America; fax 416-203-6753; website: www.tourism-toronto.com) is *the* place to go for any

Questions answered, maps provided

Official sightseeing bus

Sail the Oriole on
Lake Ontario

maps, brochures and schedules, with staff available by appointment or discussion over the telephone about places to stay, things to see and do, and special events.

Tourism Toronto also runs a year-round information kiosk, **Info TO** (255 Front Street West, Toronto Convention Centre, daily 9am–5pm). Tickets to attractions and theatre can be bought here.

Sightseeing tours

Gray Line Sightseeing Toronto (tel: 416-594-3310). A three-and-a-half hour, fully narrated bus tour, this covers all of the city's sights and attractions, including Chinatown and Harbourfront. It picks up from major downtown hotels or from the Toronto Coach Terminal.

Olde Town Toronto Tours (tel: 416-614-0999). This guided trolley-car or double-decker-bus tour covers over 100 points of interest. Tours leave daily at 9am and are two hours non-stop, or travellers are invited to see the sights at their own pace, hopping on or off at any of the 18 stops. **Toronto Harbour and Islands Boat Tours** (tel: 416-364-2412) offer the chance to see the city from the water, or for those who prefer to walk around the sights there are the **Toronto Architecture Tour** (tel: 416-922-7606) and the **Toronto Historical Board's Walking Tours** (tel: 416-392-6827).

Tax

A **Provincial Sales Tax** (PST) of 8 percent is added to goods and services. It is possible for visitors to apply for a refund, provided they have accumulated over $100 worth of receipts for non-disposable merchandise to be used outside Ontario. For further information on how to get this refund, along with a refund of the 5 percent accommodation sales tax charged by hotels, tel: 416-314-0944, or 1-800-268-3735.

The **Goods and Services Tax** (GST) is a federal tax of 7 percent charged on most goods and services sold in Canada. Visitors can claim a rebate of the GST paid on short-term accommodation for less than a month, and on many of the goods purchased to take home. For further information, tel: 1-800-668-4748 (from within Canada, toll-free) or 613-991-3346 (from all other countries).

Tipping

In restaurants the service charge is rarely included in the bill. It is customary to tip 15 percent (an easy way to do this is to match the GST and provincial sales tax on the bill, which combined total 15 percent). Taxis and limousine drivers are usually given a 10-15 percent tip. In hotels, porters generally receive at least 50 cents per bag, and room service is $1 per day per person.

Time
Toronto falls within the Eastern Standard Time Zone (Greenwich Mean Time minus five hours). From the first Sunday in April until the last Sunday in October the clock moves forward one hour for Daylight Saving Time.

Voltage
The electricity supply is 110 volts, as in the US, using two-pin plugs. Visitors from the UK will need adapters.

Opening times
Offices are generally open from 9am to 5pm, although with job-sharing and flexible scheduling some are open earlier. Government offices are usually open 8.30am–5pm.

Postboxes are red

Postal hours vary. But the main downtown Post Office at 36 Adelaide Street East is open Monday to Friday 8am–5.45pm.

Stores are a different matter altogether. Generally speaking, those downtown tend to open at 10am, while closing hours vary anywhere from 6pm to 10pm, Monday to Friday. Weekend hours change once again, with Saturdays usually spanning 9am–9pm, and Sundays (in some cases, such as the Eaton Centre) from around noon to 5 or 6pm.

Public holidays
New Year's Day (1 January), Good Friday and Easter Sunday (end of March/beginning of April), Victoria Day (fourth Monday in May), Canada Day (1 July), Civic Holiday (first Monday of August), Labour Day (first Monday of September), Thanksgiving Day (second Monday of October), Christmas Day (25 December), Boxing Day (26 December) and New Year's Eve (31 December).

Telephone
The Greater Toronto Area (GTA) is covered by two area codes, 416 and 905. Toronto has the 416 area code, while the 905 code covers the cities surrounding Toronto and other outlying areas. All calls made within the 416 area are local and do not require the caller to dial the area code. Calls made within the 905 area are not all local. If you are calling a long-distance number, dial 1, followed by the area code and then the telephone number. If you are unsure whether the number you are dialling is long distance, you can always call the operator by dialling 0. If you wish to find a local number tel: 1-555-1212 or 411 from payphones (free of charge).

Dial 411 for information

A local call from a public payphone costs 25 cents regardless of the duration of the call. Aside from cash, calling cards, prepaid telephone cards and major credit cards can all be used in public payphones, but often end up costing slightly more.

Media

Toronto has five daily English language newspapers, *The Globe and Mail*, the *Financial Post* and the *National Post* (which are national), plus the city-wide *The Toronto Star* and *Toronto Sun*. All are readily available at hotels, newsstands and corner stores throughout the city.

Home to over 300 consumer magazines and well over 100 book publishers, Toronto is the publishing capital of Canada. *Maclean's* is a weekly magazine featuring both Canadian and international current affairs. The monthly magazines *Saturday Night* and *Toronto Life* are cosmopolitan-savvy periodicals offering insight into the city's inner workings.

National and regional radio and television stations are based in Toronto, including the Canadian Broadcasting Company (CBC) which operates networks in both of the country's national languages, for radio and television, and CTV. The city also houses many multicultural, multilingual broadcast outlets, and over 65 ethnic newspapers.

For up-to-date listings and articles about the goings-on in the city, *Now* and *Eye* are good sources. Both are alternative newspaper-style magazines that are free of charge and offer comprehensive information on entertainment, music, theatre, dance, films, gallery exhibitions, dining and a wide range of other events within the city.

Good sources of information

92

Emergencies

Help is at hand

For medical, police or fire emergencies dial 911 – which is free from payphones. Foreign visitors can often find further assistance from their consulates (numbers can be found in the business section of the white-pages phone book of Toronto).

Medical assistance

All non-Canadian visitors should purchase health insurance before leaving home. Some credit card companies offer certain levels of medical or other insurance if you use their card to pay for the trip.

The following numbers could be of assistance for travellers: Canadian Medic Alert (tel: 416-696-0267), Dental Emergency Service (tel: 416-485-7121), Hospital/Dental Emergencies (tel: 416-340-3944), Hospital and Medical Insurance for Visitors (tel: 416-961-0666).

Alcohol

The minimum age for purchasing alcohol is 19. Restaurants and bars serve alcohol until 2am. Retail sales are controlled by the Liquor Control Board (LCBO) stores and The Beer Store outlets. If you are driving, place alcohol unopened in the boot of the car. If you are caught drink driving, you may end up in jail for a few days.

Accommodation

*Bed and Breakfast on
Toronto Island*

Toronto has a vast array of accommodation, particularly in the downtown area. Among the usual offerings of centrally located hotels, there are also bed and breakfasts for those looking for a more intimate option.

Tourism Toronto (*see page 89*) co-ordinates a central reservation service representing 123 member properties throughout the Toronto area.

Hotel selection

The following suggestions are listed according to three categories, based on two people sharing a room: $$$ expensive (above $180), $$ moderate ($90–180) and inexpensive (up to $90).

Four Seasons Hotel, 21 Avenue Road, Toronto ON, M5R 2G1, tel: 416-964-0411, 1-800-268-6282, fax: 416-964-2301. One of North America's top hotels, the Four Seasons is in the chic neighbourhood of Yorkville. This hotel was actually the flagship for the international chain of the same name, with spacious bedrooms adjacent to marble bathrooms and excellent service. $$$+

Four Seasons Hotel

Hotel Intercontinental, 220 Bloor Street West, Toronto, ON, M5S 1T8, tel: 416-960-5200, 1-800-267-0010, fax: 416-960-8269. Situated at the edge of Yorkville near the Royal Ontario Museum, this luxurious hotel has a swimming pool and spa/fitness facilities, along with a charming courtyard garden. $$$+

Camberley Club Hotel, 40 King Street West, 28th floor, Toronto, ON, M5H 3Y2, tel: 416-947-9025, 1-800-866-ROOM, fax: 416-947-0622. Retaining an old-world charm, Camberley Club is perched on the 28th floor of the 69-storey Scotia Plaza in the heart of the financial district. Room rates include a continental breakfast, afternoon tea, early-evening *hors d'oeuvres*, late-evening coffee and a spa/fitness centre – not to mention the spectacular views of Lake Ontario. $$$

The King Edward Hotel, 37 King Street East, Toronto, ON, M5C 1E9, tel: 416-863-9700, 1-800-225-5843, fax: 416-367-5515. Built in 1901, this elegant building is a historic Edwardian landmark with vaulted ceilings, marble pillars and marvellously opulent rooms which have recently been restored to their original splendour. $$$

Park Hyatt Hotel, 4 Avenue Road, Toronto, ON, M5R 2E8, tel: 416-924-5471, 1-800-268-4927, fax: 416-924-6693. A Toronto landmark in the hub of things at the corner of Avenue Road and Bloor Street. Its rooftop restaurant offers beautiful views. $$$

Arrival at the Royal York

Royal York Hotel, 100 Front Street West, Toronto, ON, M5J 1E3, tel: 416-368-2511, 1-800-441-1414, fax: 416-368-2884. Just a stone's throw from Union Station, this Canadian Pacific hotel is an elegant historic building that was host to the Queen of England, numerous dignitaries and Oscar Wilde when it was the Queen's Hotel. $$$

Sheraton Centre Toronto Hotel & Towers, 123 Queen Street West, Toronto, ON, M5H 2M9, tel: 416-361-1000, 1-800-325-3535, fax: 416-947-4874. Terrific locale, great views, Canada's largest indoor/outdoor swimming pool and sprawling gardens make this hotel popular with business travellers and tourists alike. $$$

Sutton Place Hotel, 955 Bay Street, Toronto, ON, M5S 2A2, tel: 416-924-9221, 1-800-268-3790, fax: 416-924-1778. Ideally located for those on business, this hotel also caters for those who enjoy the nuances of a European-like atmosphere. $$$

Crowne Plaza Toronto Centre, 225 Front Street West, Toronto, ON, M5V 2X3, tel: 416-597-1400, 1-800-268-9411 (Canada), 1-800-828-7447 (United States), fax: 416-597-8128. An upscale Holiday Inn, this 25-storey hotel is tailored for the business traveller, complete with a swimming pool and spa/fitness centre. $$

The Primrose

Best Western Primrose Hotel, 111 Carlton Street, Toronto, ON, M5B 2G3, tel: 416-977-8000, fax: 416-977-4874. Ideal for the keep-fit enthusiast, there are saunas, an exercise room and outdoor swimming pool here. $$

The Delta Chelsea Inn

Delta Chelsea Inn, 33 Gerrard Street West, Toronto, ON, M5G 1Z4, tel: 416-595-1975, 1-800-CHELSEA (243-5732), fax: 416-585-4393. A conveniently located hotel, just steps away from the downtown attractions. $$

Holiday Inn on King, 370 King Street West, Toronto, ON, M5V 1J9, tel: 416-599-4000, 1-800-263-6364, fax: 416-599-8889, reservation fax: 416-599-4785. Within close proximity of the theatre district, the hotel offers excellent views of Lake Ontario and the SkyDome from some of its rooms. $$

Novotel Toronto Centre, 45 The Esplanade, Toronto, ON, M5E 1W2, tel: 416-367-8900, 1-800-NOVOTEL, fax: 416-977-9513. Part of the international French chain, this European-style hotel is well-located, with the St Lawrence Market, financial district and Toronto's major downtown attractions all in tow. $$

Radisson Plaza Hotel Admiral, 249 Queen's Quay West, Toronto, ON, M5J 2N5, tel: 416-203-3333, 1-800-333-3333, fax: 416-203-3100. In the heart of Toronto's waterfront area, this hotel plays up the nautical theme, complete with polished brass, lacquered wood and marine art. A courtesy shuttle bus service ferries guests to and from the downtown core. $$

SkyDome Hotel, 1 Blue Jays Way, Toronto, ON, M5V 1J4, tel: 416-341-7100, fax: 416-341-5091. Built right into this famous landmark, the rooms' floor-to-ceiling windows offer a coveted view of the stadium. $$

The SkyDome Hotel

Toronto Hilton, 145 Richmond Street West, Toronto, ON, M5H 2L2, tel: 416-869-3456, 1-800-HILTONS, fax: 416-869-1420. A stately hotel in the heart of downtown's shopping district and a quick walk from the Art Gallery of Ontario, theatres and concert halls. $$

The Toronto Hilton

Toronto Marriot Eaton Centre, 525 Bay Street, Toronto, ON, M5G 2L2, tel: 416-597-9200, 1-800-228-9290, fax: 416-597-9211. Perhaps a dangerous locale for shopaholics, this hotel is actually connected to Toronto's shopping mecca, the Eaton Centre. An indoor rooftop pool and a spa/fitness centre are also present. $$

Westin Harbour Castle, 1 Harbour Square, Toronto, ON, M5J 1A6, tel: 416-869-1600, 1-800-228-3000, fax: 416-869-1420. A comfortable hotel that offers an excellent vantage point of Lake Ontario and the Toronto Islands due to its lakeside locale. Just minutes from downtown and the bustle of Harbourfront and Queen's Quay. $$–$

Hotel Victoria, 56 Yonge Street, Toronto, ON, M5E 1G5. tel: 416-363-1666, fax: 416-363-7327. Located in the heart of Toronto's theatre and financial district, this hotel is a small historic property amid the modern skyscrapers of the downtown core. $

Bed & Breakfasts

Many B&Bs are speckled throughout the city. Listed below are associations that can be contacted for information, brochures and reservations.

Bed & Breakfast Guest Houses Association of Downtown Toronto, PO Box 190, Station B, Toronto, ON, M5T 2W1, tel: 416-368-1420, fax: 416-368-1653, e-mail: bnbtoronto@powerwindows.com

Bed & Breakfast Homes of Toronto, PO Box 46093, College Post Office, 444 Yonge Street, Toronto, ON, M5B 2L8, tel: 416-363-6362.

Index